RECYCLED
CHIC

RECYCLED CHIC

AMANDA McKITTRICK

MURDOCH BOOKS

CONTENTS

ACCESSORIES AND EMBELLISHMENTS

BITS AND PIECES

INTRODUCTION

Have you ever wanted to make your own individual fashion mark without spending a small fortune? Disheartened by the uninspiring range of new fashion on offer and my tightening purse strings, I began venturing into the world of craft and vintage fashion several years ago, and it's been a wonderfully satisfying and creative experience.

Anyone can take a similar creative plunge and explore the possibilities for refashioning your own wardrobe, shop with a fresh perspective, and combine the old with the new. *Recycled Chic* will arm you with the techniques, inspiration and confidence to renew your existing clothes and accessories, or alter pre-loved fashion and fabric to suit your individual style and taste.

We are all creative at heart and enjoy having a unique style, but with our busy lifestyles, sometimes the easiest option is to buy from a typical chain store. These garments are often quite inexpensive, but frequently they're not well made and don't last long, so any pleasure they give can be all too fleeting. Often the greatest satisfaction comes from making or altering something for ourselves and sharing our skills and the things we make with others.

This book is for those among us who aren't content to look like everyone else, who dare to be a little different and show off our true personalities. When you buy second-hand or vintage, or alter your own clothes, you're easing the impact not just on your wallet, but also on the environment by **minimising** waste. As a bonus, when you buy from charity stores your money is going to those less fortunate – what better reason to get out there and reuse, revamp and restyle?

You don't need to be an experienced seamstress or pattern-maker to achieve any of the projects in this book – most of them can be accomplished with very basic sewing skills. In fact, that's the point of this book: to inspire a more free-form approach to making and remodelling clothes, rather than relying on 'traditional' sewing skills and patterns.

What's more important is a desire to explore and have fun with the many possibilities that refashioning clothes and accessories can bring. I'm living proof that the more you start to create and experiment, the more your skills and confidence will evolve. A makeover doesn't need to be radical – less is often more – but you will be noticed and admired for your originality, and without doubt you'll inspire others to follow suit. It's always great to be on the receiving end of comments such as 'I love it, where did you get that from?' It's even better when you can proudly say, 'I made it myself!'

The projects in this book are all very simple, and can be accomplished in very little time. Need a new outfit for that party or want to give a unique handmade gift? It can be as easy as changing the buttons on a jacket, taking the sleeves off a dress, shortening a skirt, or adding an embellishment to a tired old top. All the projects are quick and easy, with step-by-step photos to guide you through the basics.

As I know only too well, sometimes the hardest step can be the first one, but why not enjoy the rewards that come from being creative and start your journey today?

Amanda
X

GETTING
STARTED

SEWING KIT

It's handy to have some of these bits and pieces in your sewing kit before you start, but as you move from project to project, you will acquire a lot more along the way. I've included a list of required supplies with each project, but here's a little list that you'll find useful as you begin revamping your clothes.

- ♦ TAILOR'S CHALK (or disappearing ink marker pen) To make temporary marks on fabric, so that you know where to cut or hem or make darts.

- ♦ DRESSMAKER'S SCISSORS Reserve these for cutting fabric only, as cutting paper blunts the scissors.

- ♦ PAPER-CUTTING SCISSORS Keep a separate pair on hand for cutting paper.

- ♦ MEASURING TAPE A retractable one is handy.

- ♦ PINS Glass-headed pins are good, as they are easy to see and (unlike plastic-headed pins) they won't melt onto the fabric if accidentally ironed.

- ♦ SAFETY PINS Have a few different sizes. Large ones can be used for threading elastic through casings.

- ♦ CRAFT GLUE Available from craft and fabric stores, this glue dries invisible.

- ◆ IRON You don't need a fancy one, though a non-stick sole plate makes the task easier.

- ◆ COTTON PRESSING CLOTH To place over fabrics to protect them while they're being ironed. A clean white handkerchief or even some baking paper will do!

- ◆ SEWING NEEDLES AND THREAD Most hand-sewing needles range in size from 1 to 10. The larger the number, the finer the needle. Use fine needles for fine fabrics and thicker needles for thick fabrics.

- ◆ SEWING THREAD For most projects, a cotton-polyester blend thread will work well.

- ◆ SEWING MACHINE AND NEEDLES You don't need a fancy sewing machine. One that does straight stitch, zigzag and buttonholes will get you a very long way.

- ◆ SEAM RIPPER (UNPICKER) For easily unpicking mistakes.

- ◆ RULER For accurately marking seams and darts.

FABRIC CARE

Fabric has a wonderfully complex history dating back to the start of humankind, when natural resources such as plants and animals were the primary source of materials used to provide clothing and shelter.

Over the centuries, developments in society, technology and science have enabled the creation and refinement of the fabrics that we wear today. When you're working with fabric in the future, take a moment to consider the path that led it to you – it's truly fascinating when you delve into it! On page 140 you'll find information on various fabric types and basic care guidelines for each, but if your garment has a care label, you'd be crazy not to follow it.

As a general guide, these few tips will help you navigate the sometimes daunting task of cleaning and removing stains from fabric.

HAND-WASHING

Although it may seem tedious, hand-washing really is the best way of ensuring delicate items are not damaged in the cleaning process – it will also prolong the life of any textile, not just delicate ones. If you love that garment, care for it – so you won't have any regrets.

▸ Make sure the sink is clean.
▸ Always dissolve the detergent before proceeding. Using liquid detergent will avoid any undissolved granules remaining on the fabric.
▸ Cold or lukewarm water is best; hot water can set stains.
▸ Agitate the garment carefully by gently squeezing the fabric in the water, and gently plunging it in and out.
▸ When the water changes colour from clear to a yellowish tinge, drain the water and repeat this process until the water stays clear, adding lesser amounts of detergent each time.
▸ Rinse thoroughly, again avoiding excessive agitation.
▸ Once washed, squeeze out as much water as possible (but don't wring the garment if it's delicate). Roll the garment

in a towel to remove further moisture and lie flat on a dry towel. Or hang it to dry (with a towel underneath if you're drying indoors, to mop up drips).

‣ If hanging the garment outdoors, do so in shade – prolonged exposure to sunlight fades and weakens fabrics. The exception is white garments, as sunlight is a natural bleaching agent.

‣ Never throw delicate or woollen items into the dryer – it will spell disaster!

> *When hand-washing, it's important to be gentle, especially if you're working with fine or delicate fabrics, such as silk; old fabrics, which could be fragile; or wool, which may shrink and felt if it's rubbed vigorously or washed in hot water.*

REMOVING ODOURS AND STAINS

The best time to remove an odour or stain is right after you take the garment off. The less time you give the smell or stain to settle, the easier it will be to remove. However, if it's a second-hand garment, chances are your fabulous find has been stinky or splotched for some time.

‣ Vinegar is one cheap, easy way to remove unpleasant smells from clothes.

Add 1 cup of white vinegar to a bathtub or bucket filled with boiling water, hang the garment over it, close the bathroom door and let the steam work its magic overnight. Goodbye stench! Or, if the garment can be machine-washed, add a cup of vinegar to the load along with your detergent.

‣ Vinegar also removes some stains. Before laundering, simply dab a small amount of vinegar on the stain. This won't work for all stains, but it is a tried and true method of removing perspiration, coffee and wine stains.

‣ Wet the stain with lemon juice, or dissolve a small amount of a stain-removing product such as Napisan in a little water, then apply it to the stain. Lay the garment in the sun for half an hour and watch the stain disappear.

> *Nothing is guaranteed to remove an old stain, especially if the garment has been washed in hot water and/or ironed in the meantime (as heat will set the stain). If the stain really bugs you, think laterally – put a patch, a pocket, an appliqué or some embroidery over it, or pin a flower or brooch on to conceal it.*

ALTERING AND REFITTING

A snip here and a tuck there can transform a garment, and elevate its status from unloved at the back of your wardrobe to your new favourite piece.

Alterations can be as simple as taking up a hem, or as involved as taking apart, resizing and reassembling a whole garment.

The various techniques involved in refitting could take up a whole book, but we'll keep it simple. Keep in mind that refitting a vintage or second-hand garment isn't an exact science. It will depend on the shape and cut of the garment, your own shape and measurements, and the effect you're trying to achieve. It might involve some trial and error, pinning and repinning, and a few rounds of taking the garment off and putting it back on again, but that's all part of the fun of customising second-hand vintage fashions.

ASSESSING WHAT THE GARMENT NEEDS

First of all, put the garment on, look at yourself in the mirror and decide where it needs fixing. If you've already decided, for example, that you like the dress but hate the sleeves, remove the sleeves first then try the dress on to see how well the rest of it fits.

If the garment just needs a shorter hem, that's the easiest fix (see page 11).

For tops or shirts, or the bodices of dresses, you might need to add horizontal darts at the bust; long vertical darts that go from the bust to the waist (shown in the centre of the photo below); or tucks (shown at either side of the photo below).

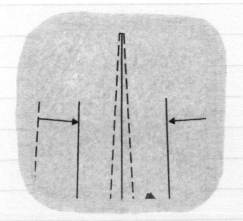

If the armholes of sleeveless tops or dresses gape, bust darts are the answer.

If the sleeves are too long or too puffy, they can be shortened and/or made narrower (see page 9).

To refit a baggy shift dress, you might need to add curved or double-ended darts (as shown in the photo below). You might need them on the front only, or on both front and back.

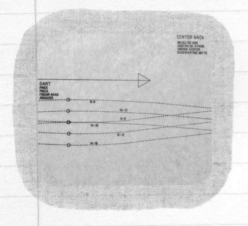

To adjust an ill-fitting dress that has a bodice and skirt attached separately, you might have to take the dress apart and adjust both pieces individually before putting it back together again.

To transform a skirt, or to make a cut-down dress into a skirt, you might need to add darts or tucks, or gather the fullness into a waistband.

MARKING ADJUSTMENTS

Once you've got the garment on, start gently pulling it this way and that to see how it changes the way the garment looks, feels and hangs. Does it look better if you pull it a bit tighter round the waist? Does the bodice sit better if you pull up the shoulders? Do the armholes gape less if you pull the fabric in a bit between the bust and underarms? Would it look better if the skirt were less full, or pleated instead of gathered?

As you go, make notes of the things that need fixing so that you have something to refer to when you take the garment off.

Using tailor's chalk (or disappearing ink marker pen), mark points at which adjustments need to be made. Take the garment off and cut or pin it according to the adjustments you've made. Put it on again and see if it looks any better. Keep going like this until you're happy with the result, then sew the adjustments in (after tacking them first if you need to – see page 19 for how to tack or baste).

ADDING SHAPE

Darts (straight or curved wedges sewn into the garment), tucks, pleats and gathers add shape to garments.

▸ STRAIGHT DARTS This is the most common kind of dart. It has only one tapered end and is used to shape fabric at the bust and waist.

▸ DOUBLE-ENDED DARTS These are mainly used in dresses. They have two tapered ends providing shaping for the bust and hips.

▸ TUCKS Tucks are folds in the fabric that are stitched into place, with the stitching running parallel to the fold. Tucks are a decorative way of adding shape.

▸ PLEATS Pleats are also folds in the fabric, but unlike tucks, they are not stitched down all the way along their length. Usually used in skirts, pleats gather in large amounts of fabric without adding bulk.

▸ GATHERS Gathers give a more relaxed look compared with pleats and tucks, yet still serve the purpose of gathering in large amounts of fabric.

LETTING OUT

Letting out a garment is a slightly trickier prospect than taking it in, as it depends on how much seam allowance there is. Check this out before you buy the garment and make sure that, once you've refitted it, there will still be an adequate seam allowance (at least 1 cm/⅜ inch). Any less than this and you run the risk of the fabric fraying and tearing if the seams strain.

Also keep in mind that letting out a very faded garment might be unsuccessful, as the seam allowance, being on the inside of the garment, will have faded less than the outside of the garment. This means that you might end up with a brighter or darker stripe of fabric down the seams or along the dart lines once you've let the garment out.

Presuming the seam allowances are generous enough to permit letting out, the following are some guidelines on how to proceed.

Tops, shirts and dresses

▸ Unpick the armhole seams and take off the sleeves.

▸ Unpick the side seams.

▸ Unpick any darts if they need to be let out.

▸ If the fabric can be ironed, press the pieces to remove the stitch marks.

▸ Sew the side seams according to the new measurements.

▸ Measure, mark and sew new darts (see opposite page) if need be.

▸ Remodel the sleeves if need be (see right), then reattach them.

Trousers and skirts

▸ Unpick the waistband.

▸ Unpick the side seams, and the back seam if need be.

▸ Unpick any darts that need to be let out.

▸ If the fabric can be ironed, press the pieces to remove the stitch marks.

▸ Measure, mark and sew new darts, tucks or gathers (see opposite page) if need be.

▸ Sew the side and back seams according to the new measurements.

▸ Reattach the waistband, or put on a new waistband.

Remodelling sleeves

▸ First, measure the circumference of the garment's armhole. Your new sleeve needs to be at least this measurement along the 'head' (its upper curved edge). Once you have this measurement, you can remodel the sleeve accordingly.

▸ If the sleeves are too wide, unpick the underarm seams and taper the width. Measure your upper arm circumference as a guide, and add at least 2 or 3 cm (an inch or so) of ease.

▸ If the sleeves are too puffy, you can both taper the width, as explained above, and reduce the puffiness by cutting the head of the sleeve in a less exaggerated curve.

▸ If the sleeves are too long, cut off the excess length, leaving enough fabric for a hem. You might need to taper the width too, as explained above.

If making bust darts, end them about 3 cm (just over an inch) away from the point of the bust. This will give a gentle curve to the bustline rather than an obvious point. When making double-ended darts, you may need to clip the fabric at the midpoint of the dart, to make the curve sit flat. If working with a heavy fabric, trim away any excess fabric along the length of the dart.

FINISHING TECHNIQUES

FINISHING RAW EDGES

It's important to finish the edges of the fabric before sewing or hemming, to stop the fabric from fraying and to achive a clean and professional look. There are a few ways to do this.

Zigzag stitch with your sewing machine.

Overlock the raw edge of the fabric.

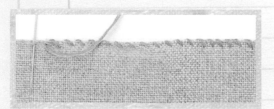

Stitch by hand using an overcast stitch (such as whip stitch, see page 21 and see above) or blanket stitch (see page 20).

Fusible tape is a godsend for delicate garments where a stitched hem would ruin the look, and is also perfect for fixing small tears or holes in fabric. It is sold in various widths and thicknesses. Applying it is as easy as turning the iron on.

USING FUSIBLE TAPE

A few things to remember before using fusible tape – wash the fabric first to remove any finishes that may prevent fusing; press the hem in place before adding the tape; and don't iron straight onto the tape, as it will stick to the iron. Instead, use a pressing cloth or just a handkerchief between the iron and the tape.

HEMMING

Taking up a hem is one of the easiest ways to alter a garment. It's worth taking care with hems as they make a big difference to how the finished or altered garment looks and falls.

Hems can be sewn by machine or by hand. Machine-sewn hems will be visible on the right side of the garment. Hand-sewn hems take longer to do but are generally neater and easier to control, especially if the hem is curved.

First, decide where the hem should fall. If you've got a friend to help you, so much the better. When levelling a hem, stand on a firm surface (not carpet) and, if possible, wear the shoes you intend to wear with the garment.

Double hem

Depending on the thickness of the fabric, a double hem gives a nice finish to the garment by hiding the raw edge. Simply turn over at least 5 mm ($\frac{1}{4}$ inch) and turn over again to the desired depth of the hem, before stitching down with your sewing machine, or by hand using the stitch of your choice (see the stitch guide on pages 16–21).

To make the double hem, fold over once and press.

Then make the second fold (over the first) and pin or baste, ready to stitch down.

Single hem

If the fabric is thick, a double hem will be too bulky, so opt instead to overlock or zigzag the raw edge. Then fold a hem into the wrong side of the fabric and sew it down by machine or by hand using using the stitch of your choice (see 16–21).

Zigzag or whip stitch the raw edge before folding over and sewing the hem in place.

Blind hem

This technique gives a very neat hem with stitching that is almost invisible from the right side of the garment. It can be used for either single or double hems.

First, measure the hem, press, then pin or baste (see page 19) to prevent the fabric from moving around when sewing.

With the wrong side of garment facing you, turn the finished edge of the fabric over approximately 5 mm ($\frac{1}{4}$ inch) and stitch horizontally through one layer then another, taking only a tiny amount of fabric each time to minimise visibility on the right side of the fabric. Check that the stitches on the front of the fabric are not obvious as you work your way around the hem. Try not to pull the thread too tightly as you go to prevent the fabric from puckering.

Hem edge turned down, being blind hemmed along the fold.

Bias binding hem

If you have almost no hem allowance to play with, bias binding is the solution. You don't need to neaten the edge first when using bias binding (although you can if you want to).

Bias binding seems a little scary at first, but once you've mastered it you'll never look back. It gives a clean finish, encases raw edges, and lies flat and smoothly around curves. It's available in a range of colours, although you can also make your own.

Bias binding can be sewn on to the right or the wrong side of the garment for different effects.

A tacked double hem, ready for blind hemming.

Open out one folded edge of the binding and fold about 2.5 cm (1 inch) of the end to the wrong side (this will create a neat join later). Match up the raw edge on the right side of your garment with the unfolded edge of the binding. Pin or baste (see page 19) in place.

Sew along the fold of the binding. Continue sewing until you reach your starting point. Allow an overlap of about 2.5 cm (1 inch). Cut the binding at an angle (to reduce bulk) and sew to the end.

Flip the binding over to the wrong side of the garment, press in place with your fingers (shaping it to the curve if there is one) and sew along the edge of the binding. Machine-stitching is quicker, but hand-sewing gives a neater finish, and also makes it easier to control the fabric, especially around curves.

Hemming stitches

SLIPSTITCH HEM

Take a small stitch through all the layers of fabric.

Pass the needle through the fold of the hem and bring it out where you want the next slip stitch to go.

SLANTED HEMSTITCH HEM

Take a small stitch through one or two threads of the fabric, then take another stitch through the fold of the hem. Repeat this along the fold of the hem, creating small slanted stitches spaced closely together. Take care not to pull the thread too tight, as the hem will pucker, but the stitches should not be too loose, otherwise the hem may sag.

MAKING YOUR OWN BIAS BINDING

Bias binding makers are nifty little gadgets, allowing you to easily make bias binding to match your fabric. Preparation can sometimes be time consuming, but it's worth it for a professional, individual look.

Binding makers come in different sizes; however, the width of binding commonly used for dressmaking is 12 mm ($\frac{1}{2}$ inch), so a bias maker of that size is useful. A thinner binding and maker should be used for lightweight or sheer fabrics.

Cut strips of fabric at double the width of the finished binding – so, for a finished width of 12 mm ($\frac{1}{2}$ inch), cut strips 25 mm (1 inch) wide.

Steps for making bias strips and binding

1 Cut the fabric across from one side of the selvedge (edge) to the other.

2 Fold the cut edge diagonally across so that it lines up against the selvedge.

3 Cut along this diagonal fold, and you'll have a starting point for marking up the strips.

4 Measure widths of 2.5 cm (1 inch) from the diagonal cut edge, marking the lines using a ruler and tailor's chalk or a disappearing ink marker pen.

5 Cut along these lines.

6 If the strips are too short, stitch two (or more) together at the ends.

7 And now, the fun part! Feed the strip evenly through the widest end of the bias binding maker and watch as the binding appears nicely folded on the other side. Magic!

Using bias binding is a great way to hem a garment that has a very scant hem allowance, as it requires only 5 mm ($\frac{1}{4}$ inch) of fabric.

OTHER TECHNIQUES

GRADING SEAMS

If the fabric is bulky, or there are several layers of fabric in the seam, you might need to grade (or layer) the seam. This involves trimming one or more layers so that they are of different widths. This reduces the bulk in the seam.

CLIPPING CURVES

Clipping a curve will remove bulk and allow the fabric to sit flat, giving the seams some ease. Make small cuts perpendicular to the seam along the edge of the curve – but don't cut into the seam, as you'll have to sew a new seam around it or replace the piece entirely... so clip carefully!

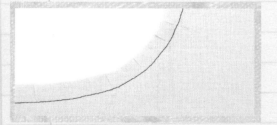

INTERFACING

Interfacing provides reinforcement, stiffening or shaping to your work, for example in collars, cuffs, buttonholes and bags. It is available as fusible or sew-in forms, in various thicknesses, and in white, grey or black. The one you choose will depend on your project, for example a lighter interfacing is suited to a lighter fabric. Always test fusible interfacing with a scrap of fabric before proceeding with the whole project, to ensure an appropriate match.

DOUBLE-SIDED APPLIQUÉ WEBBING

Vliesofix is a brand of double-sided fusible webbing with a peel-off paper back. When ironed, it fuses two pieces of fabric together permanently – imagine the possibilities! It's commonly used for appliqué work and is sold off the roll, so you can use as small or large a piece as required. Fabrics that work well with fusible webbing include cotton and cotton blends, denim, silk, wool and t-shirt fabric. Fabrics that won't work with fusible webbing are leather, velvet, and fabric that can't be ironed, such as vinyl.

BASIC MACHINE-STITCHING GUIDE

Machine sewing is fast and easy. Your machine doesn't need to be fancy – all you need for most projects is straight stitch (including reverse stitch) and zigzag. If your machine can do buttonholes or stretch stitching, so much the better, but it's not essential.

Straight stitch

This is the most basic stitch, used for seams and hems. You can vary the stitch length according to what you are sewing. In general, use a shorter stitch length for finer fabrics and a longer stitch length for thicker or heavy fabrics.

For machine tacking, use the longest straight stitch. For machine topstitching, use a small to medium straight stitch.

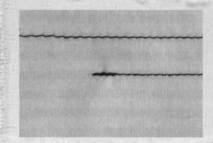

Buttonholes

Buttonholes are a variation on zigzag. Most machines will have a setting to make buttonholes automatically, some of them with just one step.

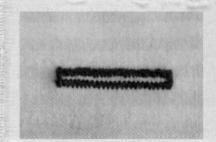

Zigzag

This sawtoothed stitch is great for finishing raw edges. The length and width of the stitches can be adjusted. Use a narrower zigzag on fine fabrics and a wider one on heavy fabrics.

When zigzag stitch is very closly packed together, it is known as satin stitch. This is useful for applique or decorative purposes.

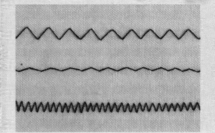

Stretch stitch

Used with knitted fabrics, this stitch stretches with the fabric.

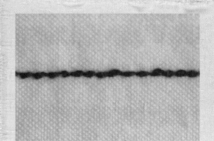

BASIC HAND-STITCHING GUIDE

While machine-sewing will always be faster than hand-sewing, it's not always easier or more convenient. Some small repairs, or those in tricky places, are easier to do by hand rather than trying to manipulate the fabric under the machine. The comparative slowness of hand-sewing also makes it easier to control the fabric and not have it careering off in all directions, as it can do if you machine-sew too quickly.

HAND STITCHES

Hand-stitching is not something to be feared – you really only need to know a few stitches for most projects and alterations. Once you get into a rhythm, hand-stitching can be very pleasurable and meditative. As your skills and confidence grow you could add some more stitches to your repertoire, but in the meantime, keep it simple and fuss free.

Some of these stitches – running stitch, backstitch and blanket stitch (among many others) – can also be used for embroidery. Or combine both hand- and machine-stitching – for example, you could machine-stitch a pocket on for strength, then go around the edge by hand using running stitch or blanket stitch for a decorative effect.

Running stitch

This the most basic hand-stitch, used for gathering, tacking, seams and mending. Running stitch is a simple in-and-out stitch, creating even spaces and stitches.

(Machine equivalent: long straight stitch)

VARIATIONS

Basting/Tacking

Long temporary running stitches are used to baste (or tack) together two or more layers of fabric. The stitches don't need to be particularly neat or even, as they will be removed once the permanent seam is sewn.

(Machine equivalent: long straight stitch)

Topstitching

Topstitching is a permanent running stitch worked along the edge of a garment, such as along collars. As well as being decorative, it helps the edge to lie flat.

(Machine equivalent: medium straight stitch)

Gathering stitch

Running stitch can also be used to gather a piece of fabric, for example for a puffed sleeve or a full skirt. If you're gathering a thick fabric, or a large expanse of fabric, it's good idea to sew two lines of running stitch for security, in case one breaks.

(Machine equivalent: long straight stitch)

Backstitch

If you don't have a sewing machine for simple stitching, backstitch is the alternative. It makes a strong line of stitching – strong enough to sew entire seams. It's also great for reinforcing areas that take a lot of strain, and for doing repairs.

(Machine equivalent: medium straight stitch)

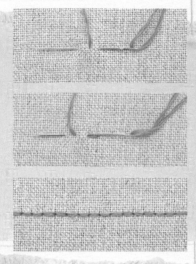

Blanket stitch

Blanket stitch is used to reinforce, as a decorative edge or to make buttonholes by hand (see page 22). It is created by pushing the needle through the fabric and wrapping the thread underneath the needle before moving to the next stitch, leaving a small gap between stitches.

(Machine equivalent: zigzag stitch)

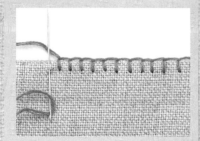

Whip stitch

This diagonal stitch along the edge of the fabric is used to join two finished edges (top right) or along a raw edge to prevent fraying (bottom right). Stitch length should depend on the thickness of the fabric – for thinner fabrics, use shorter stitches; for thicker fabrics, use longer stitches.

(Machine equivalent: zigzag stitch)

Ladder stitch

This is an alternative to whip stitch for joining two folded edges. The needle is taken along the fold of the fabric, to give an almost invisible join.

(Machine equivalent: you could use zigzag stitch, but ladder stitch is neater)

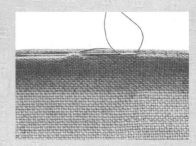

Buttonholes

You don't need a sewing machine to make a buttonhole. With a little bit of know-how you will be hand-sewing your own buttonholes in no time.

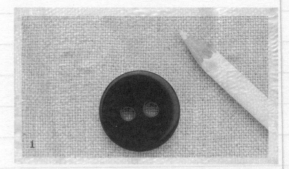

1 Measure your button and use tailor's chalk to mark the placement for the buttons on the garment.

2 Carefully cut the slits in the fabric where you made the marks. Double your thread and knot it at the end – this will provide strength and will speed up the process. Using blanket stitch, start stitching from the underside of the fabric, bringing the stitch up and back around the edge of the hole, continuing all the way around. Keep the stitches small, close together and evenly spaced. (See page 16 for making buttonholes on a sewing machine.)

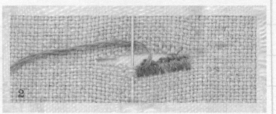

3 When you've made it all the way around the buttonhole, fasten the thread at the back of the fabric. Pass the needle under a few stitches to secure and conceal the thread and snip off the excess.

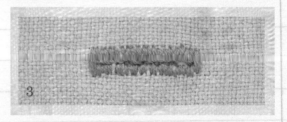

Be creative with your buttonholes and add some interest by using contrasting thread – who said buttonholes have to be boring?

notes

1 52 53 54 55 56 57 58 59 60 61 62 25 24 25 26 27

REINVENT
YOUR
WARDROBE

VINTAGE AND RETRO FASHION

For a clever and quirky wardrobe update, discover the unique and timeless appeal of bygone eras by exploring the world of vintage and retro fashion.

There are so many sources these days, the choices are seemingly infinite. Vintage and retro fashion has gained a strong popularity that is unlikely to fade any time soon, and you don't have to look far to discover a world of one-off gems.

Don't be put off by clothes that initially make you recoil, as frumpy may well be flirty in disguise. Removing or shortening sleeves, taking out shoulder pads, changing necklines, taking a dress in or up, or even just adding a belt, can be simple solutions that turn ugly into glamorous.

Think of vintage dresses as you would a bolt of fabric – if you love the fabric but hate the dress, consider cutting it up and wearing it as a skirt, a top or a scarf, or use the fabric to make a bag or other accessory. Don't be put off by the dress itself – open yourself to creative ideas and covet that one-of-a-kind fabric.

Be inspired by the styles of different eras and incorporate them into your existing wardrobe by selecting a few key items to complement more up-to-date fashion and create a look that is individual and a reflection of your personality. Wearing vintage from head to toe is often a no-no, so unless you're headed off to a fancy-dress party, opt for some signature pieces, mix the old with the new, and add a modern twist by paring it back against monochromes or wardrobe staples such as jeans.

Alterations can be the key to wearing vintage well, and giving it a contemporary makeover is not only easy but will give you the edge so often lacking in chain-store fashion. Let your imagination run free next time you riffle through racks of vintage!

WANDERING, SCOUTING AND RUMMAGING

It's always fun to go on a shopping adventure with a specific item in mind, but casual wanderings through vintage boutiques, charity stores, markets and online shopping sites can uncover hidden and unexpected gems. Inspiration might come from a wonderful piece of fabric you spot, or even from a holiday experience. Whatever the case, allowing yourself to think creatively about fashion will help you to see the many possibilities that exist.

Hunting for vintage fabric brings me true joy – it's a delight to think that a unique little piece of history can be transformed into a contemporary handmade craft project. There are a few really great online stores that I frequent, and I'm sure there are many others that remain undiscovered. Etsy and eBay are an excellent resource, but two of my favourite stores for vintage fabric are Retro Age Vintage Fabrics and Vintage Fabric Addict (see Resources information on page 150).

Shopping for vintage fabric is not limited to online, of course – markets, garage sales, charity stores and antique stores are all good places to start. Don't forget to check with your friends and relatives too; they might have suitcases and boxes of wonderful items just ready to be reinvented.

Sellers of vintage fabric these days will bundle up a bag of scrap fabric for you, but if you're anything like me, you've already got a pile of it lying around. Scrap fabric is ideal for smaller projects such as covering buttons, fabric rosettes, bows, bookmarks, phone cases, greeting cards or little gifts for friends – there are many creative ways to put those remnants to good use.

01 man-shirt makeover 1

Need a cool quick fix for a summer's day? Raid a man's wardrobe or make a beeline to the shirt section in your local charity store – second-hand shirts are cheap and the selection is always diverse.

WHAT YOU NEED

▸ MAN'S LONG-SLEEVED SHIRT
▸ FINE CORD OR 2.5 CM (1 INCH) WIDE RIBBON (for the belt and shoulder straps)
  For the belt you will need enough to go around your waist twice, tie in a bow and hang loosely.
  For the shoulder straps you will need 1.5 m (50 inches). This can be shortened later if need be.
▸ SCISSORS
▸ SEWING MACHINE (or sew by hand if you prefer)
▸ NEEDLE
▸ THREAD
▸ SEAM RIPPER/UNPICKER
▸ PINS
▸ MEASURING TAPE
▸ TAILOR'S CHALK/DISAPPEARING INK MARKER PEN

HOW TO MAKE IT

BEFORE

1

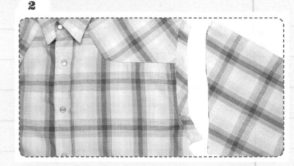

2

1 Using the seam ripper, carefully unpick the pocket(s) and iron both shirt front and pocket(s) to get rid of the holes left by the stitching. Keep the pocket(s), you'll use them later.

2 Cut off the sleeves as shown in the photo, leaving 2 cm (¾ inch) of sleeve outside the armhole seam edge to allow for hemming.

3 Cut off the top of the shirt, 4 cm (1½ inches) above the second button from the top.

4 Hem the edges of the armholes by turning the fabric under twice and straight-stitching along the existing seam line.

5 To create the casing for the shoulder strap, turn the top raw edge 1 cm (⅜ inch) over to the wrong side, then turn it over again by 5 cm (2 inches), press and straight-stitch across. Do this first on the front of the shirt, then repeat on the back.

6 Feed the shoulder strap through the front and back of the casing using a safety pin attached to one end as a guide (see tip box, opposite). Try the top on, adjusting the straps on the shoulders so that they look and feel right. Secure with a firm knot and cut off the excess length. Wriggle the knot down into the casing so that it doesn't show. Alternatively, leave the excess length, tie it in a bow and wear it as a feature.

7 Try the shirt on and pin the pocket(s) in position (just one or both, it's up to you). Straight-stitch (see page 16) around the two sides and bottom edge, leaving the top open. If the pocket has a flap that you want to use, attach the pocket itself, sewing down one side, across the bottom and up the other side, then attach the pocket flap, sewing along the top only. (Alternatively you could create pockets from scrap fabric as an interesting feature.) Tie the belt around your waist and you're ready to stay cool while soaking up the sun.

3

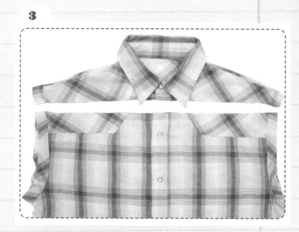

4

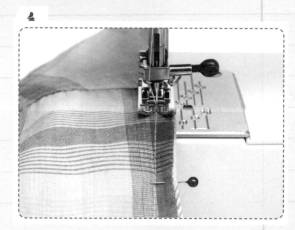

5

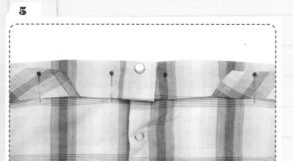

7

6

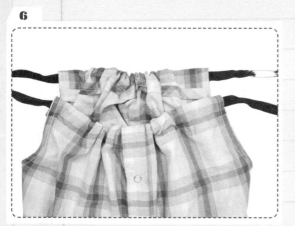

To thread a cord or elastic through a casing, you can either attach a safety pin to one end and push it through the casing, or use a small metal device that will grab the cord or elastic and hold it while you pull it through.

Shirring is a great little technique to have in your sewing repertoire. It's easy, and once you get the hang of it, it's addictive – you'll want to shirr everything in sight. Shirring involves using elastic thread to gather rows of fabric; the result has lots of give as well as a pretty gathered effect.

Shirring adds shape and detail to ill-fitting garments and can add a creative edge to anything from a t-shirt to a sack-like dress.

Once you've mastered the basics, think about shirring in a different way – shirr the back or bodice only, or add a shirred ruffle down one side or to the collar.

Experimentation is the key.

Refashioning a man's shirt is not only fun, it's also incredibly cheap (this shirt cost me almost nothing) and easy to achieve.

WHAT YOU NEED

- MAN'S LONG-SLEEVED SHIRT
- SEWING MACHINE
- SCISSORS
- THREAD
- PINS

- SHIRRING ELASTIC
- SPARE BOBBIN
- SEAM RIPPER/UNPICKER
- MEASURING TAPE

- TAILOR'S CHALK/DISAPPEARING INK MARKER PEN
- BUTTONS (if you want to replace the existing buttons on the shirt)

HOW TO MAKE IT

BEFORE

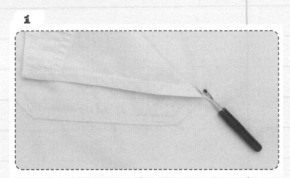

1 Using the seam ripper, carefully unpick any pockets and iron the shirt to get rid of the holes left by the stitching. Discard the pockets.

2 Draw a line across the width of the shirt, just beneath the armholes. Cut along the line. The bottom piece of the shirt will become your top. From the upper piece of the shirt, cut the arms off and keep them to one side (you'll use these for straps later). Discard the rest.

3 Unbutton the shirt. Make a 1 cm (³/₈ inch) double hem (see page 11) on the top (cut) edge of the lower piece.

4 On a spare bobbin, hand-wind the shirring elastic until the bobbin is full. Don't stretch the elastic as you go, just wind it loosely. Don't try to wind the bobbin using the machine – hand winding is the way to go here. It won't take long, I promise!

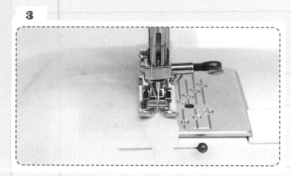

5 Load the bobbin with the elastic into your machine, just as you would normally, and you're almost ready to sew. Do a test on a scrap piece before you get started – use the discarded top half of the shirt and sew a few rows (see opposite tip box for shirring pointers).

6 Starting on one side of the button strip, and finishing up on the other side of the button strip, begin straight-stitching (see page 16) 5 mm (¼ inch) from the top, stretching the fabric out as you go. Then line the edge of the presser foot up to the last stitched row, and sew another five rows, stretching the fabric out as you go.

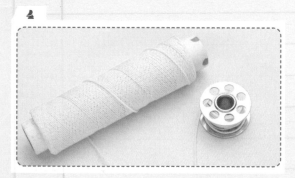

7 Try the top on, and mark the spot under your bust that you think looks right. Mark a line across with pins or tailor's chalk, and sew a line of shirring (see opposite tip box) along this line.

5

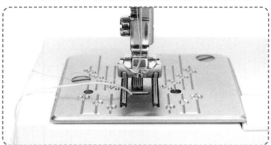

6

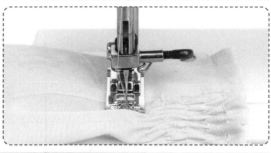

SHIRRING TIPS

- *Don't forget to forward and reverse stitch at the end of each row of stitching so the elastic doesn't unravel.*
- *Use a longer stitch length, plus you may have to play with the stitch and tension combination to get it right. You've got it right when the fabric stretches out to its original length without sliding along the rows of shirring.*
- *Always sew with the right side of your garment facing up, as you want the elastic to be on the underside.*
- *Cut off the elastic at the end of each row.*

7

8

10

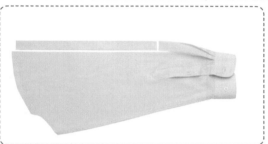

9

8 Sew another two rows of shirring under this, and try it on again. Decide whether you want the next three rows to be above this row, or below it (the degree of puffiness up top will be reduced if you sew the rows higher), and continue sewing. Alternatively, sew the entire bust section with shirring. With the iron set to medium, blast some steam over the rows of shirring and watch the elastic tighten up. You'll still be able to stretch the fabric out, this just tightens and neatens your rows up. (Note that you're holding the iron above the fabric to steam it, not actually ironing it, which will flatten the shirring.)

9 Try the shirt on again and mark any points between the buttons where gaping is an issue. Hand-sew some snap closures at these points to stop any gaping.

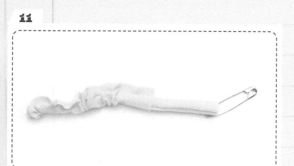

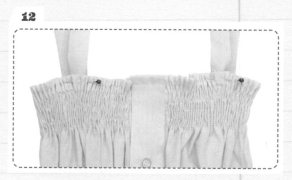

10 Make the shoulder straps from the sleeves. Fold each sleeve in half along the top edge. From this top edge, cut a strip 2.5 cm (1 inch) wide when folded (so the piece is 5 cm/2 inches wide in total).

11 Fold one piece with right sides together and stitch 5 mm (¼ inch) in from the edge. Attach a safety pin to one end and feed this through the tube. This will turn the tube the right way out as you go.

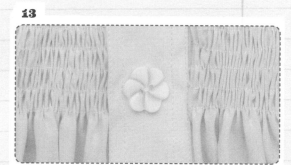

12 Try the shirt on once more and mark the placing for the straps. Cut off the excess length and double-hem the raw edges, then stitch them in place.

13 Add buttons of your choice, or leave them as they are. Now it's pleasure, not business, as you breeze through summer in your refashioned man-shirt.

03 scarf halter-neck top

Inexpensive vintage scarves are plentiful and can be found in a wonderful selection of colours and designs. But why be limited to wearing them around your neck?

Two scarves can become a slinky halter-neck top. Cinch it at the waist or wear it loose and billowy – it'll look great with a pair of skinny jeans, can be layered for the more modest among us, and as an added bonus it'll hide a multitude of sins yet still remain provocative ... perfect for a night out on the town.

HOW TO MAKE IT

1. Press both scarves flat. Cut the long rectangular scarf in half lengthways. For the neck strap, with the fabric wrong side facing up, fold over 1 cm (½ inch) along both long edges to neaten. Measure the halfway point along one of the long edges. Measure the width of your neck and mark this on the strip also, using the halfway point of the strip as the halfway point of your neck measurement.

BEFORE

2 Gather-stitch (see page 19) along one edge of the square scarf, then gather in the folds to the neck measurement marked on the neck strip.

3 Lay the gathered square scarf (right side up) on top of the opened-out neck strap, matching the measurements, and placing it so that the top edge sits about 1 cm (½ inch) above the lower folded edge of the neck strip. Then fold the top edge of the strip down, sandwiching the gathered edge as shown, and making sure that the folded edges of the strip meet neatly. Pin at right angles (so the machine can run over the top of them), then straight-stitch (see page 16) along the long edges, leaving the short ends open for now. At this point, tie it around your neck and determine whether you want to wear the top with a belt, or loose with the tie at the bottom. If you want to wear it with a belt, follow steps 4 and 6. If you want to wear the top loose, follow steps 5 and 6.

4 To make the belt, fold the waist strap in half with right sides together and the edges matching up, pinning as you go. Straight-stitch 5 mm (¼ inch) in from the edge, along the entire length. Attach a safety pin to one end and feed this through the tube. This will turn the tube the right way out as you go. Press the strip flat with an iron. Trim the ends as needed, then fold about 1 cm (³/₈ inch) at each end to the inside of the tube. Straight-stitch across the ends.

5 To wear the top loose with the tie at the bottom, lay the longer strip flat with the wrong side facing up. Fold both long edges over 1 cm (½ inch) to neaten. Mark the halfway point along one long edge. Mark the halfway point on the wrong side of the lower edge of your scarf, too. Before you stitch the pieces together, try the top on for length, and shorten if necessary by folding up the bottom of the scarf on the wrong side to see how it looks, then cutting off the excess before you sew the bottom strip in place. When you're happy with the length, lay the scarf over one edge of the strip, matching up the two halfway points. Fold the other long edge of the strip over, sandwiching the scarf inside the strap and making sure the edges of the strap meet neatly. Pin together, then straight-stitch close to the edge of the strip.

6 Try the top on, tying the neck strap so that the top sits comfortably and looks good, then decide whether you want to trim excess length off the ends of the neck strap. Trim as needed, then fold about 1 cm (³⁄₈ inch) at each end to the inside of the tube. Pin, then stitch the ends closed.

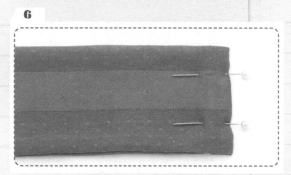

If you wear the top with the tie around the waist, but find that the top slips and exposes more of you than you're comfortable with, you could always secure the tie to the back edges of the top with a few discreet stitches.

04 sassy strapless top

Gorgeous fabric but an ugly dress? Cut the bottom half off and wear the rest as a top – a new outfit in a flash.

Keep your eyes peeled for dresses in charity stores that have the potential to be worn this way – you just never know what you might find. Choose a dress or skirt with an elastic waist, and try it on around your bust, ensuring a snug fit. A loose-fitting elastic is to be avoided if you plan to wear this strapless!

Mix and match belts or straps to give your top a completely new look each time you wear it.

WHAT YOU NEED

- ▸ **DRESS OR SKIRT** with an elastic waist
- ▸ **SEWING MACHINE**
- ▸ **SCISSORS**
- ▸ **THREAD**
- ▸ **NEEDLE**
- ▸ **PINS**
- ▸ **MEASURING TAPE**
- ▸ **TAILOR'S CHALK/DISAPPEARING INK MARKER PEN**

If the top is too long, measure the length you want, allowing 2.5 cm (1 inch) for the hem, cut it across the bottom and finish with a double hem.

If the dress came with a sash, like the one pictured, recycle the sash for your top, or join strips of the leftover fabric from the top of the dress to make a sash or belt (or straps if you prefer not to go strapless).

HOW TO MAKE IT

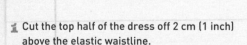
BEFORE

1. Cut the top half of the dress off 2 cm (1 inch) above the elastic waistline.

2. If the dress has a lining, remove it by either unpicking or cutting just below the elastic, taking care not to cut into the outer fabric. This will remove bulk from your soon-to-be-top.

3. Fold the cut edge over 1 cm (½ inch) to the wrong side, then fold it again to enclose the raw edge, and pin it in place. Hem 5 mm (¼ inch) from the top all the way around, stretching the fabric out and holding it taut as you go. Tie on the sash and you're done!

05 ruched t-shirt

Plenty of us have t-shirts in our wardrobes that are functional but boring – and while they're too uninspiring to wear, it seems a waste to throw them out.

With just a piece of elastic, you can spruce up a tired old t-shirt and give it a new look. This is also a great treatment for t-shirts that are otherwise fine, but are just a bit too long.

WHAT YOU NEED

▶ T-SHIRT
▶ SEWING MACHINE
▶ SCISSORS
▶ THREAD
▶ THIN ELASTIC – a piece the same length as your t-shirt
▶ PINS
▶ MEASURING TAPE
▶ TAILOR'S CHALK/DISAPPEARING INK MARKER PEN

HOW TO MAKE IT

BEFORE

1

2

1 If you don't like the sleeves and/or the collar of your t-shirt, cut them off (t-shirt fabric won't fray, so there's no need to add a hem).

2 Mark a straight line down one side of the front of your t-shirt, in line with the point of your bust from the side seam.

3 Cut along the marked line.

4 Turn the t-shirt inside out, match up the cut edges and pin together. Starting from the top, zigzag stitch (see page 16) all the way along the two edges.

5 Pin the elastic to the top of the zigzag seam, and holding it taut, sew a straight stitch down the centre of the elastic and all the way along the seam. Keep stretching the elastic as you go, as this is what will create the ruche. Snip off excess elastic, and turn your t-shirt the right way out. Voilà, one resplendent ruche!

notes

06 daring décolletage v-neck dress

Dare to bare your décolletage by altering a dress into a v-neck. It's a great way to refashion a stuffy and unbecoming neckline.

Necklines can be altered in many ways – a plunging v-neck may not appeal to the more modest among us. If that's you, cut the V a bit higher, so it doesn't reveal too much. Other options are to add a lace collar or a ruffle, or bind the neck edge with fancy ribbon or a fabric to complement the dress design.

WHAT YOU NEED

▸ VINTAGE OR OLD DRESS
▸ SCISSORS
▸ THREAD
▸ BIAS BINDING (see glossary)
▸ SEWING MACHINE
▸ 1 M (1 YARD) OF RIBBON, about 2.5 cm (1 inch) wide
▸ PINS
▸ MEASURING TAPE
▸ TAILOR'S CHALK/DISAPPEARING INK MARKER PEN

HOW TO MAKE IT

1 If the dress has sleeves, cut them off. Also cut off the collar and/or any neckline facings or binding, depending on what the dress has. Unpick the shoulder seams, if need be, to separate back from front entirely. If the dress has a collar, removing it will remove the facings and/or binding on the back of the dress too; if this is the case with your dress, you will need to apply bias binding to the back of the dress also (using the same technique as in steps 3–5).

2 Try on the dress and mark the V shape with a ruler, remembering you will lose 1 cm (½ inch) more for the hem. Make sure both sides are even by measuring either side from the edge of the fabric. Cut the V out of the fabric. Stay-stitch the neck edge (see Glossary); this prevents it from stretching, which will cause the V to gape.

3 Cut the bias binding 5 cm (2 inches) longer than the neck opening. Open out one folded edge and pin it to the right side of the dress, matching up the raw edges. Fold under about 1 cm (½ inch) at the beginning and end of the binding to neaten it. Pin the binding all along, allowing a bit extra at the point of the V and making a small tuck in the binding at this point (this will help it fold over to the back more neatly later).

4 Straight-stitch (see page 16) along the fold in the bias binding, being careful not to stretch the bias or the neckline as you go.

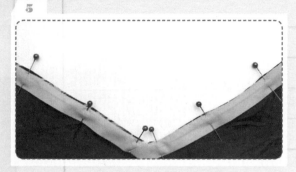

5 Flip the binding over to the wrong side of dress. Snip through both dress and binding at the point of the V, snipping up to – but not through! – the stitching. Pin the binding down and sew the binding to the dress, close to the edge. Do this by hand using slipstitch (see Glossary) for the neatest finish.

6 Bind the armhole seams using the same technique, beginning and ending the binding at the underarm side so it is less visible.

7 Cut the ribbon into four equal lengths. Fold the top edges of the shoulders down to hide the raw edges. Fold the ends of the ribbon down too, to enclose the raw edges, and pin the folded ends to the top of your dress. Stitch them on, then finish the free ends of the ribbon by folding them under twice and stitching across. Now put the dress on, tie the ribbons and admire your pretty décolletage!

Match the fabric of the bias binding to the fabric of your dress: for a cotton or linen dress, use a cotton or polycotton binding; for a silk, satin or polyester satin dress, use a satin bias binding.

07 sleeveless dress

Love the dress but hate the sleeves? Removing sleeves can transform a dress from dowdy to striking in no time. Using bias binding to finish the armholes is the quickest, easiest method and will give a clean, professional look. No need to complicate things with fancy armhole facings – simply stitch on the binding and you're good to go!

If your dress has long sleeves, and you don't want to remove them completely, consider shortening them (use the excess fabric to create a cute cuff), or cutting them off just below the underarm seam to create a capped sleeve.

WHAT YOU NEED

- DRESS WITH SLEEVES
- SEWING MACHINE
- PINS
- THREAD
- NEEDLE
- SCISSORS
- BIAS BINDING (see Glossary)
- IRON
- SEAM RIPPER/UNPICKER

HOW TO MAKE IT

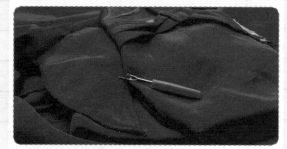

1 Turn the dress inside out and using an unpicker/ seam ripper, remove the shoulder pads (if the dress has them).

2 Using an unpicker/seam ripper, remove the sleeves. You've survived the tedious part, now it's time to transform!

3 Cut the bias binding long enough to go around the edge of the armhole, plus about an extra 2.5 cm (1 inch) for overlap. Turn the dress right side out. Open out one folded edge of the bias binding. Fold under about 1 cm (½ inch) at one end of the binding. Starting at the side seam, pin the bias binding along the armhole edge, with the right side of the binding facing the right side of the dress, and making sure the two edges match up. Straight-stitch (see page 16) along the fold of the bias binding. When you get to the end, allow 1 cm (½ inch) or so overlap. There's no need to fold under the second end of the bias binding, as this will be concealed. Flip the bias binding over to the wrong side of the dress and press it in place (with the iron if the fabric will stand it; otherwise just run your finger along the seam line to flatten it a bit and shape it to the curve).

4 There are two options for finishing the binding: If your dress is made from a delicate fabric and you feel that a seam along the armhole edge will ruin the look of it, hem the edge by hand. To do this you will need to take a small stitch in the garment, making sure your needle doesn't go too far though to the right side of your fabric, and then stitch through the edge of the binding, continuing all the way around. Make sure not to pull the stitches too tightly, to avoid puckering. Patience will be required; however, you'll have a lovely clean finish on the right side of your dress!
If your dress isn't so delicate and you don't mind the look of an armhole seam, straight-stitch by machine just in from the edge of the bias binding. Baste the binding to the dress first if you feel this will make the sewing easier.

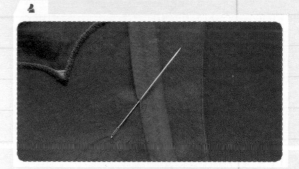

Using bias binding is a great way to hem a garment that has a very scant hem allowance, as it requires only 5 mm (¼ inch) of fabric.

CONTRAST BINDINGS

Another option is to attach the bias binding to the wrong side of the dress at the armhole edge, then fold it over to the right side so that the binding becomes a feature. (You could also bind the neck edge in the same way for a matchy-matchy look.)

Use regular bias binding, or patterned or satin binding, in either a matching or a contrasting colour, depending on the fabric of the dress and the look you're after.

If you have enough leftover fabric from the dress, you could use that to make your own bias binding (see page 14).

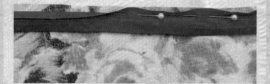

Pin the right side of the binding to the wrong side of the garment, then sew along the fold.

Neatly sew the binding down on the right side of the garment.

08 backless summer dress

Love that cute summer dress but feel a little too hemmed in? Take to the back of it with a pair of scissors and a shape in mind, and breathe a whole lot easier.

Try on your dress and decide what shape you want to cut out of the back. Arch shapes work well, but a love-heart or an oval can also be a pretty option.

WHAT YOU NEED

▸ DRESS WITH HIGH BACK and without a zipper at the back
▸ SCISSORS
▸ THREAD
▸ BIAS BINDING IN MATCHING COLOUR
▸ SEWING MACHINE
▸ TISSUE PAPER OR TRACING PAPER
▸ PENCIL
▸ FRENCH CURVE/SEAMSTRESS CURVE (see glossary) – if you don't have one you can use a compass or trace around a dinner plate or the like, or just opt for freehand
▸ TAILOR'S CHALK/DISAPPEARING INK MARKER PEN
▸ MEASURING TAPE
▸ PINS

HOW TO MAKE IT

BEFORE

1. Have a friend mark the points at the waistline and the neckline where you'd like the shape to sit – it's better to cut on the conservative side to avoid having your whole back on display. Remember, too, that once you've attached the binding the cut-out area will end up slightly larger all round, so allow for that. If you don't want your bra straps visible, plan the design accordingly. Lay the dress out flat, then pin a piece of tissue or tracing paper over the top of it to draft your pattern. From the points you've marked on the dress, draw two lines on the paper running parallel across the top and bottom, adding 5 mm (¼ inch) for seam allowance. Draw a line down the centre. Between these lines and from the centre line, draw a curve on one side. Remove the paper, fold it in half on the centre line, and cut along the curve. You will now have a symmetrical template.

2 Position this template in place on the back of the dress, and pin it in place.

3 Trace it, then cut out the shape.

4 Cut a piece of bias binding to go around the curved edge, plus about an extra 2.5 cm (1 inch) for overlap. Open out one folded edge of the bias binding. Fold under about 1 cm (½ inch) at one end of the binding. Starting on a straight part (not a curve), pin the bias binding all the way around the curved edge of the shape, with the right side of the binding facing the right side of the dress, and making sure the two edges match up. Cut another piece to go along the straight edge, plus about an extra 2.5 cm (1 inch) for overlap. Pin it in the same way as you pinned the piece along the curved edge.

5 Straight-stitch (see page 16) along the fold of the bias binding. At the corners, make sure the needle is down in the fabric, then lift the presser foot and pivot the dress to align the next part of the seam correctly. Clip the curves of the fabric slightly (see page 15), so it lies flat when you stitch the binding along the raw edge. Also clip the corners, and trim off any excess binding at the ends of the pieces. Turn the dress inside out. Flip the bias binding over to the wrong side of the dress and press (with the iron, if the fabric will stand it; otherwise just run your finger along the seam line to flatten it a bit and shape it to the curve). Straight-stitch along the edge of the binding either by machine or by hand to secure it in place. Press the edges of the cut-out shape again on the wrong side, to make sure they lie flat.

Now wear your dress with cool confidence!

4

5

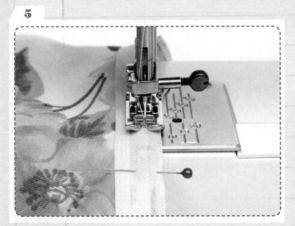

Here the binding is sewn first to the right side of the garment, then finished on the wrong side, so that it doesn't show. Alternatively, you can apply the binding to the wrong side of the fabric, then fold it over to the right side. This gives you a contrasting edge that can make an attractive feature.

Another quick change you can make to your dress, if it is too long, is to shorten it (see page 11). Depending on how much fabric you cut off, you could always use the excess to make a ruffle, if you wanted.

09 shapeless to shirred

Although the dress in this project looked fine before I took to it with shirring elastic, it didn't suit my shape – the top half was boxy and unflattering. As mentioned in the man-shirt makeover project on page 33, shirring is a wonderful way to quickly add shape or transform a dress, skirt or top.

Be creative with the straps by using ribbon, bias binding or contrasting fabric, or make the shirring a feature by using a contrasting thread colour. See page 35 for shirring tips.

BEFORE

HOW TO MAKE IT

 If the dress has a zip, unpick it and remove it.
Sew up the zipper opening.

2 Try the dress on and make a mark on the fabric where you'd like the top of the transformed dress to be. Add 1.5 cm (⅝ inch) for the hem, then cut off the shoulders and neck of the dress. Zigzag along this raw edge, then hem it with a single hem (see page 11).

3 Now for the fun part – shirring! On a separate bobbin, hand-wind the shirring elastic until the bobbin is full. Don't stretch the elastic as you go, just wind it loosely. Don't try to wind the bobbin with the machine, as this will stretch the elastic. Load the bobbin with the elastic into your machine, just as you would normally, and you're almost ready to sew. Do a test on a scrap piece before you get started – use the discarded top part of the dress as your practice fabric and sew a few rows.

4 Start stitching 5 mm (¼ inch) from the top, and go all the way around. When you get to the end, forward and reverse stitch so the elastic doesn't unravel. Cut off the elastic at the end of each row. Sew the entire bust section with shirring, trying the dress on at intervals to determine how many rows will look best. When you're finished shirring, fold the ribbon in half and stitch the fold to the inside of the dress at the centre front. Tie it around your neck, and you're done!

Be sure to try the dress on first to ensure a loose enough fit around the bust, as this will tighten and gather in when shirred. You'll also need to be able to get the dress on over your head with the zip done up, as you will be removing the zipper later.

notes

10 classic woollen capelet

Make a statement and achieve an elegantly classic look at the same time by cleverly altering an outdated woollen skirt. Capelets are not only fashionable, they are also functional – warding off the mid-season chills when it's too mild for a coat yet still too cool to go out without some sort of cover-up.

WHAT YOU NEED

- ▶ A SKIRT (see tip box on page 67)
- ▶ SEWING MACHINE
- ▶ SCISSORS
- ▶ NEEDLE AND THREAD
- ▶ EMBROIDERY OR UPHOLSTERY THREAD
- ▶ BUTTON
- ▶ TAILOR'S CHALK/DISAPPEARING INK MARKER PEN
- ▶ PINS
- ▶ SEAM RIPPER/QUICK UNPICK

HOW TO MAKE IT

BEFORE

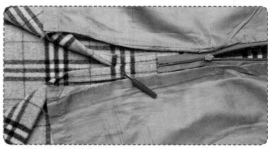

1

2

1 Turn the skirt inside out and unpick the zipper and the entire length of the back seam. If the skirt is lined all the way to the bottom edge, then keep the lining; if it's only lined halfway, then unpick the lining too.

2 Wrap the skirt around your shoulders with the opening facing the front. Fold the waist to the underside of the skirt, and adjust until you are happy with the length that the capelet will be, keeping in mind you'll need about 8 cm (3 inches) at the top (not including the waistband) to gather for the collar. Mark the folded edge in place with pins.

3 Lay the fabric out with the wrong side facing up and cut the waistband off at the point you've marked and discard. Zigzag along the cut edge on the skirt to stop any fraying.

4 Double-hem the two edges you removed the zip from.

5 Make sure the folded edge at the top of the capelet measures 8 cm (3 inches) from the fold to the zigzagged edge. Thread the needle, knot the end of the thread, and starting from the inside of the fabric, run a gathering stitch (see page 19) approximately 2.5 cm (1 inch) from the zigzagged edge, all the way along, pulling in the fabric loosely as you go. A big gather looks better – stitches about 2 cm (⅝ inch) long and 2 cm (⅝ inch) apart. Keep the stitches neat and even, as they will be visible on the finished cape. Before you tie off the thread at the end, make sure the gather isn't too tight. Try the capelet on to see if it looks right.

6 While you've got the capelet on and mark the spot where you'd like the button to sit. Sew the button on. On the other edge of the capelet, in the matching position, mark a buttonhole. Make the buttonhole by machine or hand (see page 22). Or, if your buttonholing skills aren't great either way, you can fasten the cape with a square of Velcro and just add the button for embellishment.

3

4

5

6

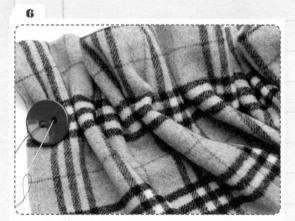

Choose a skirt made from a thick fabric such as wool, tweed or gabardine. Try the skirt over your head and pull it down over your shoulders with the zip undone and facing the front – this may sound weird, and you may want to do it in the privacy of a changing room to avoid any bewildered stares. If this fits snugly or loosely from the zip down, then it will be fine to convert into a capelet – if it's too tight, I suggest trying a skirt that's a little larger.

Customise your capelet even further by stitching ribbon, lace, or ricrac to the edges, or use fusible webbing to iron on some vintage doily details. Instead of a button you could use two pompom ties – see page 100 for instructions on how to make them.

11 sweet skirt

Too often vintage dresses look great on the rack, but quite frumpy when you try them on. Sighs of 'if only' can be a thing of the past, simply by cutting the dress in two!

Be on the lookout for stunning fabrics and designs – it's surprising what you can find with this project in mind. A dress without a waistline is ideal, but not essential – think beyond the dress and imagine a sweet skirt. It doesn't matter if the dress is too big on you, as the excess fabric will be gathered into the waistband. Use any leftover fabric to make a scarf, a fabric flower embellishment or a bow.

Warning: this may become an addiction!

WHAT YOU NEED

- VINTAGE DRESS – one without a waistline is ideal
- SEWING MACHINE
- THREAD
- SAFETY PIN
- SCISSORS
- THREAD
- PINS
- TAILOR'S CHALK/ DISAPPEARING INK MARKER PEN
- MEASURING TAPE
- 2.5 CM (1 INCH) WIDE ELASTIC for the waist (cut a piece long enough to go around your waist and allow about 5 cm (2 inches) extra for overlap)

BEFORE

HOW TO MAKE IT

1 If the dress has a zip, unpick it and remove it.

2 From the bottom of the dress, measure up to where you'd like the skirt to sit at your waist and add 7 cm (2.5 inches) for the seam allowance. Mark this measurement with a pin, take the dress off and draw a line across the width. Now cut! And say goodbye to that daggy old frock. If need be, sew the bottom part of the zipper opening closed.

3 Fold the waistline over 1 cm (½ inch) to the wrong side and press, then fold over 5 cm (2 inches), press and pin. This will be enough of a casing to thread the elastic through. Sew a straight stitch (see page 16) nearly all the way around, 5 mm (¼ inch) from the fold, then again 5 mm (¼ inch) from the top of the waistline. Leave a 2.5 cm (1 inch) gap at the back, so you can feed the elastic through.

4 Attach a safety pin to the end of the elastic, to make it easier to feed the elastic through the casing. Thread the elastic through, right around and back out of the same gap again, making sure that it doesn't twist. Try on the skirt and mark the elastic where it feels comfortable. Double-check that the elastic hasn't twisted. Overlap the two ends of the elastic and stitch together (zigzagging back and forth a few times is a good method). Finally, stitch closed the gap in the casing by hand or machine, and your skirt is ready to wear.

If you're not keen on elastic waists, you could always insert a zipper into the back seam and then gather the fabric into a waistband. Make the waistband from excess fabric from the top of the dress, or from a contrasting fabric.

2

3

4

notes

12 denim mini-skirt

A denim salute to Levi Strauss, who started the manufacture of jeans way back in 1853. What was initially designed for workers in factories has become a much-loved staple in many of our wardrobes. As fashion rapidly evolves, so do the styles of jeans on the market, so what was cool a couple of years ago might now look a little dated. I'm sure I'm not the only person to have more than one pair of unworn jeans in my closet.

This project is tried and true, and remains a favourite for fashion DIY-ers. Like jeans themselves, the denim mini is here to stay. It can be dressed up, dressed down, dressed right down, and customised in so many different ways. Fray it, stud it, paint it, embroider it, patch it with vintage fabric, cut the waistband off and stitch on a vintage scarf as a new waistband, or use a vintage scarf as a belt – the possibilities, are endless.

WHAT YOU NEED

- JEANS
- TAILOR'S CHALK/ DISAPPEARING INK MARKER PEN
- SEWING MACHINE
- NEEDLE
- THREAD (try to match it to that used in the seams of the jeans)
- SCISSORS
- UNPICKER
- PINS
- MEASURING TAPE
- VINTAGE SCARF (optional)

HOW TO MAKE IT

BEFORE

1. Try on your jeans and mark the length you'd like your skirt to be, allowing a little bit extra for the hem if you don't want a frayed edge. Don't worry if it looks too long at this point – it's always better to shorten the skirt later than to cut it too short initially. Cut the legs off at this mark, and set them aside – you will need them later.

2 Unpick one inner leg seam, starting from the bottom of the zipper and continuing along on the inside of one leg. Do the same for the other inner leg seam.

3 Turn the jeans over and, starting at the crotch, unpick the centre back seam to just below where the curve of the seam starts.

4 Turn the jeans right side out and flatten them out (iron them if need be). Overlap the front crotch seam so the denim sits flat, and pin in place.

5 Do the same to the back. You'll now have a big gap in the middle of both front and back – don't worry about it for now, as it will be filled in later. Try the skirt on to check that you're happy with the flare of it – if not, then adjust the pins.

6 Stitch down the edge of your seam, sewing over the existing seam of the jeans. Start at the zip and work down to the bottom of the centre seam. Repeat this on the back, starting from the top and sewing to the bottom along the centre seam.

7 Cut two sections of the leftover leg fabric, each slightly larger than the gaps in the skirt. Don't worry about cutting neatly, as you will trim them later. To cover the gaps, pin one section in place under the front of the skirt, and the other under the back. Stitch these pieces to the skirt, again starting at the top of the gap and working your way down along the existing seams.

9 Turn the skirt inside out, cut off excess fabric from underneath and neaten up the bottom edge. Zigzag along the edges of the inserted piece as far as you can go to prevent the edges from fraying. If you want frayed edges, wash the skirt and throw it into the dryer. When it comes out, the edge will be tangled with longer threads – cut the tangles off and you'll have a nicely frayed edge. If fraying is a little too casual for you, hem the bottom edge to the desired length. Thread the vintage scarf through the loops as a belt, or take it one step further if you wish and add a decorative edging such as lace or ribbon.

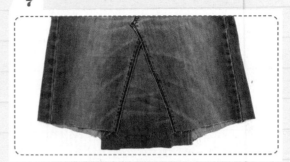

If hacking up your old favourite pair of jeans is a little daunting, buy a pair from a charity store for next to nothing and use them as a test. For a longer skirt, choose baggier jeans – the longer your skirt, the more fabric will be required to fill the gaps.

ACCESSORIES
& EMBELLISHMENTS

EMBELLISHMENTS

Whether it's bows, blooms, sequins, feathers, pins, beads, buttons, ribbons, ricrac or lace, embellishments add a little something extra to your outfit. They take virtually no time to make or to apply and usually cost very little. Many embellishments also have the added benefit of being easily removed and worn in different ways.

Take time to rummage through your favourite trinkets and consider how you might use what you already have in another way. Delve a little more deeply next time you're at a market or charity store for bits and pieces that can be reworked and refashioned to suit your style.

Restyling vintage finds or existing garments can be as simple and inexpensive as changing the buttons on a cardigan or shirt, adding a few beads in strategic places, or brightening up monochromes with splashes of vibrant colour in the form of a fabric flower or decorative trimming. Immerse yourself in the recesses of your local craft store and survey the many embellishments and trimmings on offer – you'll emerge inspired and brimming with ideas.

QUICK EMBELLISHMENT IDEAS FOR THE CRAFTER ON THE GO

▸ *Dress up a plain t-shirt with a lace trim or collar.*

▸ *Add interest to a hat by attaching faux flowers to a ribbon band or pins.*

▸ *Stitch sequins onto a pair of ballet flats.*

▸ *Add lace to a pair of cut-off shorts.*

▸ *Thread a long, fine chain through the top of a tassel and wear it as a necklace.*

▸ *Sew some ricrac to the hem of a collar, sleeves or skirt.*

▸ *Replace buttons on a cardigan or jacket with some cute vintage finds.*

▸ *Add a length of chain to either side of a bow and wear it as a necklace.*

▸ *Tie a bow to the side of a multi-stranded bead necklace.*

▸ *Use fusible webbing to attach a section of a doily to a cut-off shirt cuff.*

ATTACHING EMBELLISHMENTS

APPLIQUÉ

Applying appliqué is very simple, and can be done quickly. Pin the appliqué shape to your garment, and stitch around the edges using tiny slip-stitches (see Glossary on page 146). Add a few extra stitches across the middle part of the appliqué if you feel it's not sitting right.

BEADS

Beads can be bought in a wide range of shapes, sizes and colours. Attaching them is easy with a little patience and know-how. If you have a design you wish to bead, then draw the outline lightly onto the fabric with tailor's chalk.

To sew on individual beads, thread a needle with a thread to match the colour of your fabric, and knot the two ends together – sewing with a double thread will add strength.

Starting on the underside of the fabric, push the needle through to the right side and thread a bead onto the needle.

Insert the needle back into the fabric to create a backstitch (see page 20) the length of your bead. Bring the needle out again some way ahead of the bead you just placed, and stitch the next bead on in the same way. Continue in this manner for all the beads.

SEQUINS

Sequins are available in trims, fringes, lines of overlapping discs, or separately. If you want the sequins to be connected or to run closely together, buy and attach them in strips. Otherwise, buy them separately and attach each one individually.

Sequins can be attached using a hot glue gun or by stitching them on. Gluing is a quick and easy technique for those that don't like to sew; however, sewing them on, although time consuming, will ensure they remain in place longer.

To sew on individual sequins, start by threading a needle with a short length of thread that matches the colour of the sequins (or use clear thread), and knot one end. From the underside of the fabric, push the needle through the fabric where you'd like the sequin to sit, thread the sequin onto the needle and, holding it in place against the fabric, pull the thread through.

Insert the needle into the fabric close to the edge of the sequin, and pull the thread tight. Repeat to attach more securely, and continue attaching sequins in this way. Using a shorter length of thread will ensure that you won't have to replace too many sequins should the thread break.

To stitch on strips of sequins, simply tack (see page 19) the strip to your garment to hold it in place, then working from the back of the fabric, stitch to the garment, making sure you catch the thread holding the sequins together as you go.

13 leather and ribbon belt

Cinch your waist in style with a braided leather and ribbon belt. Customise it differently each time you wear it by using a clip-on embellishment such as a flower (see project on page 93) or bow.

Use leftover scrap leather from the clutch project on page 126, or buy a scrap piece from a fabric or craft store. As an alternative to leather, you could use a strip of fabric that won't fray, such as felt, velvet, synthetic suede or a stretch fabric.

WHAT YOU NEED

- **STRIP OF SOFT LEATHER** measuring 7.5 cm (3 inches) wide and three-quarters of your waistline measurement (see tip box on page 85)
- **SEWING MACHINE**
- **TAILOR'S CHALK**
- **MEASURING TAPE**
- **SCISSORS AND/OR CRAFT KNIFE OR SCALPEL** (to cut the leather)
- **LEATHER NEEDLE** (if hand sewing; or use a sewing machine)
- **1 M (1 YARD) OF RIBBON**
- **THREAD**
- **EMBELLISHMENT** – a fabric flower or a vintage brooch with a clip is ideal
- **CLIP (OPTIONAL) AND CRAFT GLUE** (if your chosen embellishment doesn't have a clip)

HOW TO MAKE IT

1 On the wrong side of the leather strip, mark two lines 2.5 cm (1 inch) in from either side, and starting and ending 2.5 cm (1 inch) from either end.

2 Cut along these lines, making sure you don't cut right to the ends, as you want to keep the leather in one piece.

3a

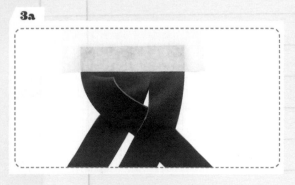

3 Tape one end to a table and begin braiding. Now, this step requires a bit of concentration and focus! Bring the left strip over the centre, then the right strip over the centre (3a), then the left strip over the centre again (3b). Feed the bottom of the strip through the gap on the right side from back to front or front to back (3c). Continue this in reverse order (right, left, right, bottom goes through left gap). Continue to the end of the strip, and if you've done this correctly, the bottom should be free of tangles (3d). If you do have any tangles, you'll have to start over again ... don't say I didn't warn you!

3b

3c

3d

2 Cut the ribbon into two equal lengths. Position one piece at either end of the leather braid, to the wrong side (4a). Fold the two sides of the leather over the ribbon, and stitch this together with the wrong side facing down to prevent the leather from being scratched by the machine's feed dogs (or alternatively use a walking foot on your machine if you have one) (4b). Fold the loose end of each piece of ribbon over a couple of times and straight-stitch across to neaten the ends.

This project can be easily adapted to make a headband or a wristband, too – just measure around your head or wrist and cut the length of leather and ribbon to size, using a thinner width for a more delicate look.

4a

4b

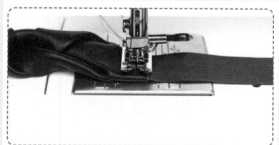

14 ribbon and lace belt

Add a hint of girlish charm with a ribbon and lace belt – a delicate and pretty combination that's easily achieved with an iron and a pair of scissors. Indulge your creative side and spend some time exploring the many types of lace and ribbon combinations on offer at your local craft store.

WHAT YOU NEED

- ▶ A LENGTH OF RIBBON – decide whether you want it to sit high around your waist or lower around your hips. Allow 4 cm (1½ inches) extra to this measurement for the hem at each end.

- ▶ A LENGTH OF LACE the same length and width as the ribbon
- ▶ A STRIP OF VLIESOFIX the same length as the ribbon
- ▶ COTTON PRESSING CLOTH (see Glossary) or baking paper

- ▶ SCISSORS OR CRAFT KNIFE
- ▶ NEEDLE
- ▶ THREAD
- ▶ HOOK AND EYE CLASPS

HOW TO MAKE IT

1. Choose your ribbon and lace combination – lay the lace on top of the ribbon to determine a good fit and colour match.

2. Cut a strip of Vliesofix and lay it flat on your ironing board, with the textured side up. Position the piece of lace, right side up, on top of the Vliesofix strip. Press with a dry iron on medium heat – first, make sure you cover the whole piece with either baking paper or a thin piece of cotton fabric to prevent any adhesive from sticking to the iron.

3. Peel the backing off the strip of Vliesofix, and cut off any straggly bits of adhesive with scissors or a craft knife.

4. Lay the lace (Vliesofix side down) over the ribbon. When you're satisfied with the positioning, press again with a cloth or baking paper placed over it. The lace and ribbon will now be fused together.

2

3

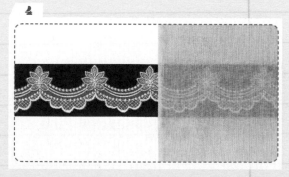

1

4

5

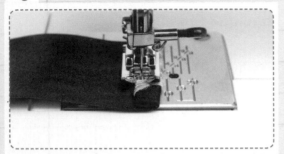

6

Frog closures are ornamental closures that are both functional and decorative, and can be found in all sorts of shapes, sizes and designs, from tiny embroidered fabric frogs to large Swarovski crystal-encrusted sparklers. Use one of these to add some real personality to your belt.

5 Hem the ends of the ribbon to stop any fraying. To do this, fold over 1 cm (³⁄₈ inch) at each end, then repeat to make a double hem. Stitch into place.

6 Sew hook clasps to one end of the belt at both top and bottom, match up with eye clasps on the other side, and stitch these in place.

notes

15 softly gathered scarf

Tired of trying to tie your scarf so it sits just right? Give your scarf a quirky edge by adding a gather and a cute button – problem solved!

Rectangular scarves will work best for this project, but square scarves are not off limits – be brave and experiment with the technique to achieve a one-off neckpiece. Now who said scarves were complicated?

WHAT YOU NEED

- ▸ LONG RECTANGULAR SCARF (narrow if possible, see tip box on the opposite page)
- ▸ TAILOR'S CHALK
- ▸ SEWING MACHINE
- ▸ MEASURING TAPE
- ▸ SCISSORS
- ▸ NEEDLE
- ▸ EMBROIDERY THREAD
- ▸ BUTTON

HOW TO MAKE IT

1

{ BEFORE }

2

1 Measure about 25 cm (10 inches) from both ends of the scarf. Measure and lightly mark a horizontal line between these two points, along the middle of the scarf. Using embroidery thread neatly gather-stitch (see page 19) along this line, gathering the folds loosely. Before you cut the thread and fasten it off, try the scarf on to see if you're happy with the way it's sitting – if it's too tight, then ease the folds out along the thread a little. When it looks right, fasten the thread with two or three small backstitches (see page 20), but don't cut the thread.

2 Using the same length of thread, sew the button to one end where the thread starts and in the centre of the scarf. Match up the ends of the scarf and mark the point where the buttonhole will be. Make the buttonhole with the sewing machine or by hand (see page 22).

A scarf with angled ends is best for this project, but they're not always easy to find. If yours doesn't have angled ends, you could cut them at an angle and hem the edges, or just leave them as is if you're happy with squared-off ends.

16 vintage silky scarf flower

Not all of us like to wear scarves around our neck. Why not convert a silky vintage beauty into a beautiful bloom and parade it as a brooch, a bag pin, a shoe clip, or attached to a ribbon as a corsage around your wrist?

This project is perfect for scarves that may be damaged or stained, as you will only need one thin strip. Carefully wash your scarf before you begin, or disguise any marks in the way you choose to roll the fabric up.

WHAT YOU NEED

▸ VINTAGE SCARF – it can be square or rectangular, as long as the rectangular isn't too long
▸ SMALL PIECE OF FELT
▸ PIN (such as a brooch pin, safety pin or shoe clip)
▸ SCISSORS
▸ NEEDLE
▸ THREAD

HOW TO MAKE IT

1 Cut a 10 cm (4 inch) wide strip off the scarf, from one edge to another. Fold this strip in half lengthways, with the wrong sides together.

2 Knot one end of the thread, and sew a line of a running stitch 1 cm (3/8 inch) in from the raw edge, from one end of the strip to the other. The stitches should be roughly 2 cm (3/4 inch) apart, although precision isn't vital here.

3 Holding the needle end of the thread, gather up the fabric along the thread loosely. Tie off the thread to hold your gather together.

If the ends of the strip are frayed, turn them under and stitch them down before you fold and roll the strip.

4 Roll the gathered fabric up until you reach the end. Roll it with the prettiest side of your fabric inwards, as this is what you'll see when the flower is unfurled.

5 Stitch through the fabric at the bottom of the raw edge, to secure the folds and prevent it from fraying. Trim any frayed threads off. Unfurl your pretty bloom!

6 Add beads or buttons if you wish, by threading from the bottom and up through the centre of the flower. Cut a small circle of felt and glue to the bottom of the flower. Allow the glue to dry, then glue on a clip.

When choosing a scarf for your flower, find one that's made of a soft fabric that will gather easily into pretty, soft folds. A crisp cotton just won't give the right effect for this project.

notes

17 tie rosette

Most men will have ties in their wardrobe that they no longer wear – or shouldn't be allowed to wear. Spirit one away and give it a new lease of life by rolling it up into a lovely little rosette.

Charity stores are also a goldmine for ties – selections range from vintage right through to last week's designs, and they are usually inexpensive. Roll one into a rosette and pin it to a top or a bag to add a bit of creative flair.

WHAT YOU NEED

▸ MAN'S TIE
▸ SCISSORS
▸ CRAFT GLUE
▸ BROOCH PIN

This technique is not limited to ties – use any scrap of fabric, or experiment with inserting a layer of lace to give it a completely different feel. See the shoe-clip project (page 116) for a rosette made from scrap fabric.

HOW TO MAKE IT

1. Add a drop of craft glue to the skinny end of the tie.

2. Fold the end over.

3. Begin rolling the tie up, rolling it over onto itself a couple of times.

4. Twist it twice and roll it onto itself again.

5 Dab some craft glue on the underside of the fabric to secure it as you go.

6 Keep rolling the fabric around, twisting where you think it needs it, and adding a drop of glue to secure it each time.

7 When your rosette has taken shape to your liking, snip off the end and fold it to the underside.

8 Add a few drops of glue. Pin in place while it dries.

9 Once the glue is dry, remove the pin and glue or sew a brooch pin to the back.

notes

18 fluffy pompoms

Have a ball with scrap wool and create some delightfully cute, fluffy and inexpensive pompoms.

There's no denying that pompoms add a dash of colour and frivolity to anything you choose to adorn. Add them to scarves, beanies, berets, gloves, bags, even shoe-clips (see page 116) – bunch them up together or hang them individually. Combine yarns of different colours or textures, or use yarn with metallic thread or feathery bits woven into it for a unique effect.

WHAT YOU NEED

▸ SCRAPS OF YARN
▸ CARDBOARD (reuse a cereal box, a tissue box, or rummage through your recycling bin)
▸ SCISSORS
▸ YARN NEEDLE
▸ COMPASS, or a circular item of the diameter you want your pompom to be which can be traced around

You can also get pompom makers from craft stores. These are a speedy alternative if you want to make a lot of pompoms.

HOW TO MAKE IT

1 On a piece of cardboard, draw or trace two circles the diameter that you wish your final pompom to be. Use a compass if you have one, or simply trace around the edge of a round object you have in your home. The one pictured measures 5 cm (2 inches) across. Draw smaller circles (half the diameter of the larger ones) inside the larger circles.

2 Cut around the outer and inner circles to make two doughnut shapes. Cut a piece of wool 30 cm (12 inches) long, and sandwich it between the two pieces of cardboard. Later you will use this to secure the middle of the pompom.

3 Cut a few manageable lengths of wool (an open arm's length is good, otherwise you may get in a tangle) and with your fingers, start winding it through and around the centre hole. Keep winding around the ring until you run out of wool, and start again with another piece when you do. Any straggly bits can be evened up at the end.

4 As the layer of wool thickens and the centre hole becomes smaller, use a yarn needle to thread the wool through.

5 When the centre hole is filled, use a pair of sharp scissors to cut through the wool and between the two pieces of card – this requires a bit of patience, as the layers will take a bit of snipping to get through. When you've cut the whole way around, pull on the centre thread, winding it round the centre of the pompom a couple of time for extra security. Tie a firm knot to secure, and trim off any straggly bits. Secure the pompom to your project by weaving, tying, stitching or gluing on the tail.

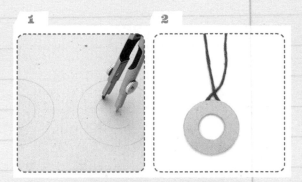

19 customised buttons

Covering buttons with scrap fabric helps to use up all those small offcuts, and is also a quick and easy way to add detail to an outfit.

Buttons can be worn in so many ways – as earrings, brooches, bobby pins, added to a jacket or cardigan, even threaded together as necklaces, bracelets, bag embellishments – the options are only limited by your imagination. Match buttons to an outfit, wear them as a contrast, package them up and give them as gifts, or store them in jars for future use. Good things come in small packages!

WHAT YOU NEED

▸ BUTTON (a button with a shank is ideal, but you can also use this technique to cover a button with holes)
▸ SCRAP FABRIC (find a piece that is at least double the size of the button)
▸ NEEDLE
▸ SCISSORS
▸ EMBROIDERY, UPHOLSTERY OR NYLON THREAD (it needs to be stronger than ordinary sewing thread)

HOW TO MAKE IT

1 Position the button onto the section of fabric that you like the most.

2 Measure from the centre to the edge of the button. Mark this distance onto the fabric, all the way around the outer edge of the button, and draw a circle. (It doesn't have to be a perfect circle, as the fabric will be gathered up later.) If you're using a button-making kit, trace the template supplied.

3 Cut this circle out.

4 Run a small gathering stitch (see page 19) all the way around the fabric circle, close to the edge, leaving a tail at the start.

5 With the wrong side of the fabric facing up, place the button in the centre. Pull the two ends of the thread up tightly, tie a knot and trim the excess thread. If you are covering a button without a button-making kit, try not to cover the shank or the holes, so you can still push the needle and thread through!

6 If you're working with a kit, now is the time to seal up the back. Take the back piece of the button, and with the serrated edge facing the fabric, push down on it firmly to secure in place. If you need to, use the end of a thread spool for a little extra pressure.

1

2
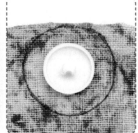

3

4
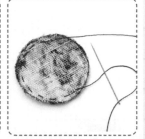

5

6

customised buttons (four simple button ideas)

Button bobby pins, hairbands and earrings are small but sweet ways of uplifting an outfit.

Glue your button to a bobby pin (choose the type that has a flat round disc for attaching embellishments to), or stitch some to an elastic headband for a quirky one-off look.

Need the perfect pair of earrings to match an outfit and want something original? Cover buttons and glue them to findings (which are readily available in craft stores online, in a variety of styles and metals). Glue a stud finding to the back of a button, or glue the button to an ornamental bezel – the combinations of fabric and setting can produce some stunning results.

Mark your page in style with a button bookmark! Cover the button and glue it to a bookmark finding. Alternatively, sew some vintage buttons to a strip of vintage fabric with pinked, zigzagged or blanket stitch edges. Bookmark findings have a round flat disc that you can stick buttons or other embellishments onto, and are available in different styles and sizes – online suppliers are your best bet.

Another way to use scrap fabric in a bookmark is to glue a strip of fabric under a glass cabochon. Glass cabochons can be bought online or at craft and beading stores.

These instructions are for making buttons without a kit. If you'd prefer to use a kit, button-making kits can be found in most craft stores. They're inexpensive, and will come with templates for cutting your fabric. If you have a kit, then you can bypass step 2 on page 103 and use the supplied template instead.

If you wish to cover more than one button and you're not using a button-making kit, cut a template out of paper to save time and make your job easier.

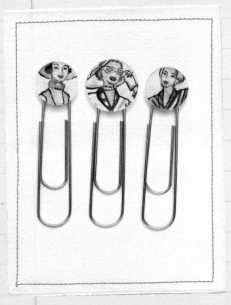

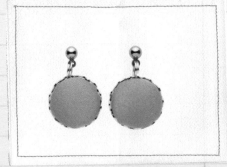

20 lacy-glam doily earrings

Doilies are back! No longer only found gathering dust on nanna's sideboard, they've re-emerged in retro-cool craft. Crocheted doilies can be snipped and shaped into a range of accessories, worn as embellishments to add a feminine touch, and best of all, you can buy them for next to nothing in charity stores.

Keep an eye out for delicate, smaller circles and chandelier shapes within the larger doily – they're perfect for a pair of glam earrings. Doilies can become the basis for statement pieces or delicate and subdued accessories – once you start looking at doilies in detail, you'll notice many shapes that will add the right touch of vintage glamour to any outfit.

WHAT YOU NEED

- ▶ CROCHETED LACE DOILY
- ▶ SCISSORS
- ▶ FABRIC STIFFENER (available at good art and craft stores, or online)
- ▶ BAKING PAPER
- ▶ SMALL PAINTBRUSH
- ▶ PAIR OF EARRING HOOKS

HOW TO MAKE IT

1 Press the doily if it's creased. Look closely at the doily and the shapes that you're wanting to cut out. Cut carefully around the shape, being careful not to cut into any of the lace that joins parts of the shape together.

2 Lay the shapes on a piece of baking paper, and paint both sides with fabric stiffener, ensuring that the lace is saturated. Leave to dry on a flat surface – this may take a few hours. As the lace dries, turn the shapes over and flatten them out.

3 Once dry, trim off any straggly lacy bits, and your doily is ready to hang from an earring back. Stick a hook through a tiny hole at the top of the lace and squeeze gently to ensure it won't slip out.

If big dangly earrings aren't your thing, glue a brooch pin to the back, or attach a chain to the doily shape and wear it as a necklace instead (see page 108).

Add a bit of sparkle to your doily earrings by dangling some small, lightweight beads from the edges off small jump rings, or stitch them through the lace of the doily. For a different look, stitch a design into the lace using contrasting thread.

1

2

3

21 vintage doily necklace

Give an unloved crocheted lace doily a new lease on life with a couple of snips and a delicate chain, and wear it as a one-off necklace to dress up a plain neckline. Hunt for unusual shapes and sizes, or reuse a shape that you cut out for the earring project on page 106.

Use a chain from a necklace that you no longer wear, or find a cheap one in a charity store. Chains with pendants are perfect, as it's simply a matter of removing the pendant and replacing it with the doily – no need for extra jump rings or clasps. In addition, you can repurpose the pendant as a brooch – two pieces of jewellery from one!

WHAT YOU NEED

- CROCHETED LACE DOILY
- JEWELLERY PLIERS
- CHAIN – if the chain doesn't have a pendant you will also need two jump rings (available from craft and bead stores)
- FRAY STOP (or a similar product that, when painted onto raw edges, will stop fabric from fraying)
- BROOCH FINDING (optional)

HOW TO MAKE IT

1. Look closely at the doily and cut out the shape you want, being careful not to cut into any of the lace that joins parts of the shape together (see photos on page 107). Paint any loose threads on the edges with Fray Stop.

2. If your necklace has a pendant on it, detach it at the connecting jump rings by pulling them apart gently using a pair of jewellery pliers. If your chain isn't connected to a pendant, open up a link in the chain and attach a jump ring to each end.

3. Thread the jump rings through holes in the doily, then squeeze the jump rings closed with the pliers.

4. If you now have a pretty pendant with no chain, glue a brooch finding to the back of it.

22 headbands

Channel your inner goddess and emphasise your luscious locks with the charming allure of a handmade headband. With flirty feathers or luxurious sparkles, practical or a fashion statement, a simple headband can inspire and transform.

WHAT YOU NEED

▸ HEADBAND – If making the feather headband, a fabric headband is best, though plastic will work too. For the sparkly headband, use a plastic, fabric or elastic headband
▸ FEATHERS OR BEADED APPLIQUÉ
▸ CRAFT GLUE, or needle and thread if you have an elastic headband

HOW TO MAKE IT

1 To make the feather headband, lay the feathers out to get an idea of how you'd like them to be positioned before you begin. Attaching the feathers to a headband is as easy as adding a spot of glue to the feather and sticking it to the headband, layering them as you go. Allow to dry before wearing it or your feathers may fly!

2 There are two options for attaching a beaded appliqué to a headband. If your headband is plastic, run a small strip of craft glue down the centre of the back of the appliqué. Position it on the headband, pressing down firmly, and set it somewhere safe to dry. If you have an elastic headband, use a needle and thread to stitch the two together. Work from the underside of the appliqué, making small stitches in the elastic and along the centre back side of the appliqué. Secure with a double stitch and a small knot at the end.

Fashionable feathers have a long and fascinating history, and notably rose to prominence in early 20th century when Parisian cabaret dancers adorned their costumes with flirtatious plumes. Styles may have changed over the years, but rather than falling out of fashion, feathers have taken flight in high-end fashion collections. Feathers lend an air of sophistication and vintage glamour – look no further than fascinators, corsages, dresses, earrings, and of course – the headband. Feathers can be found in a wild array of colours and sizes – opt for small, earthy, neutral toned feathers or stand out from the crowd with a brightly coloured plume.

1

2

23 no-sew bow

What could be better than a project that doesn't require sewing? No fiddling with thread and needles ... just a few folds and a dab of glue, and you have a feminine fabric bow to add a romantic touch to a headband, a bag, a dress, a belt – let your imagination and style dictate.

These instructions are for a bow measuring 5 cm x 10 cm (2 inches x 4 inches). What size do you want your bow to be? Take this measurement, double it (in both height and width), and cut your fabric to size – the same instructions apply.

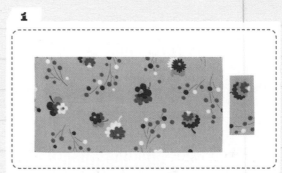

WHAT YOU NEED

▶ SCRAP OF FABRIC
▶ SCISSORS
▶ CRAFT GLUE
▶ IRON
▶ RULER
▶ PENCIL
▶ PINS
▶ BROOCH CLIP

HOW TO MAKE IT

1 Cut a strip of fabric 10 cm x 20 cm (4 inches x 8 inches). Cut another strip of fabric 2.5 cm x 5 cm (1 inch x 2 inches).

2 Take the larger strip and with the wrong side facing you, fold the top long edge in to the middle of the strip and press with an iron. Do the same for the bottom long edge. Repeat these instructions on the smaller strip.

3 Take the larger strip again and fold one end in to the middle and press. Fold the other side end in to the middle and press.

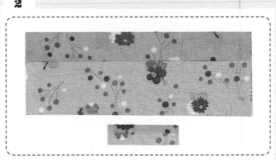

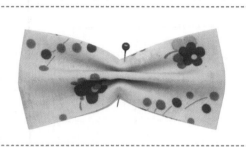

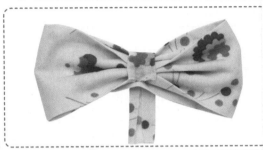

4 Pinch the larger strip together in the centre and adjust the fabric until you are happy with the gathers. Pin, to secure.

5 Turn the larger strip over so the back is facing up. With the wrong side facing down, secure one end of the smaller strip to the centre of the back of the larger strip, using a dab of craft glue.

6 Wrap the smaller strip around the front of the bow, cut off and fold under the excess fabric at the back, and secure this in place with another dab of craft glue. Pin it to keep it in place until the glue dries.

7 Attach to a hairclip, an alligator clip, a headband or a brooch pin using craft glue.

notes

24 shoe clips

Transform the look of a favourite pair of shoes with the help of two little clips. Embellish the clips in any way you like to create several looks, by attaching bought objects such as ribbon, lace, feathers, or fabric, or things you've made yourself – pompoms (see page 100), buttons (see page 102) or bows (see page 114). A quick wardrobe fix and a snap to make!

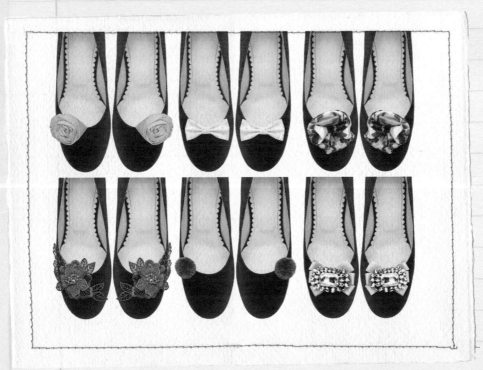

HOW TO MAKE IT

1 Cut a small piece of felt and glue this to the flat part of the shoe clips. Let the glue dry before doing the next step.

2 Glue the embellishment (pompom, bow, flower, etc) to the felt on the shoe clips, and set aside while the glue dries. If the embellishment can't be glued, attach with a few stitches on to the felt instead. Clip on to your shoes and step out in style.

1

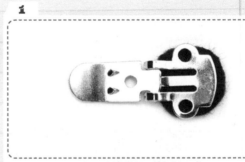

2

25 reversible shoe bag

Sling your spare shoes over your shoulder in style, protect them in transit, and keep dirt off your clothes with a chic shoe bag. If the shoe fits, bag it!

As a bonus, the bag's reversible. Of course it's not just suited to shoes – it's great for lingerie or craft supplies, or make a smaller version to carry your make-up.

The bag in the photo was made with vintage sheeting fabric, though you could use a blanket, tea (dish) towels, pillowcases, upholstery or drapery fabric – whatever washable fabric takes your fancy!

WHAT YOU NEED

- ONE PIECE OF OUTER FABRIC
  measuring 40 cm x 95 cm
  (15 inches x 38 inches)
- ONE PIECE OF LINING FABRIC
  measuring 40 cm x 95 cm
  (15 inches x 38 inches)
- 1.5 M (1½ YARDS) RIBBON,
  2.5 cm (1 inch) wide
- SAFETY PIN
- THREAD
- SEWING MACHINE
- TAILOR'S CHALK/DISAPPEARING
  INK MARKER PEN
- MEASURING TAPE
- SCISSORS
- PINS

HOW TO MAKE IT

1 Press both pieces of fabric with an iron. Sew a 1 cm (³⁄₈ inch) double hem (see page 11) on the long edges of both pieces of fabric. Fold the lining piece in half widthways, with the wrong sides together. Pin along the sides, and stitch together 1 cm (³⁄₈ inch) in from the edge, stopping 6 cm (2½ inches) from the top raw edge.

2 Repeat step 1 on the outer piece. Once you have stitched together the sides of the outer piece, turn it right side out and insert it into the lining piece, which should still be inside out.

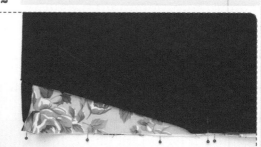

3 Pin the top edges of the lining and outer fabric together, first on one side of the bag and then the other. Straight-stitch (see page 16) across, 1 cm (³⁄₈ inch) from the top. (Note that in this step you are sewing only two layers of fabric (one layer of lining, one layer of outer fabric) together at one time – not all four layers. If you do that you will sew your bag closed!)

4 Zigzag the raw edges, then turn the whole thing right side out through the side gap.

5 Straight-stitch 1 cm (³⁄₈ inch) down from the top edge on both the front and back of the bag. Measure 4 cm (1½ inches) down from this seam, just above the level of the side splits, and stitch another line across on both front and back (just above the level of the side splits), to create the casing for the ribbon. To feed the ribbon through the casing, attach a safety pin to one end of the ribbon and push the safety pin through the casing. Cut the ribbon to your desired length and tie a knot in the end.

26 classic ring-handled bag

Whip up a gorgeous-ring handled bag in the time it takes to write your shopping list. Be on the lookout for charming vintage handles in your travels. It doesn't matter if they're attached to a bag you don't like – you can easily cut away the bag and reuse the handles. Popular styles include bamboo, bakelite, beaded, and plastic in varying colours and sizes.

Before you start on your bag, think about when you might use it the most – will it be a shopping bag, a work bag, or a little summery evening bag? Find fabric to suit the look you're after, and if you feel that it needs a bit of extra pizazz, customise it with embellishments – fabric flowers, applique, or vintage buttons are all cute additions.

I used some vintage fabric for this version. Consider using upholstery fabric, drapery, or old linen or blankets – make your choice of fabric something special and unique.

WHAT YOU NEED

▶ FOR THE OUTER FABRIC, use either two pieces each measuring 38 cm x 45 cm (15 inches x 18 inches), or one piece measuring 45 cm x 95 cm (15 inches x 37 inches). If you're using offcuts you might have to use two pieces. Using one large piece of fabric means you get a continuous pattern going from the front to the back of the bag, and you don't have to hem to lower edge.

▶ PIECE OF LINING FABRIC 45 cm x 95 cm (15 inches x 37 inches)

▶ SEWING MACHINE

▶ SCISSORS

▶ NEEDLE

▶ THREAD

▶ ROUND BAG HANDLES

▶ PINS

▶ MEASURING TAPE

▶ TAILOR'S CHALK/ DISAPPEARING INK

These instructions are for a bag measuring 40 cm (15 inches) high x 36 cm (14 inches) across the bottom. You can make the bag whatever size you want – just remember to add 1 cm ($\frac{1}{2}$ inch) to the sides and bottom, plus an extra 5 cm (2 inches) to the top for the handle casing.

HOW TO MAKE IT

1 Cut the fabric to size, then press flat with an iron. To make the lining, with wrong sides facing, pin the lining piece(s) together. Measure and mark a spot 20 cm (8 inches) from the top on each long edge. If you want the bottom of your bag to have curved corners, like the one pictured, draw a curve on either edge (measure both to make sure they're even – you can trace around a cup or glass to get a nice smooth line).

2 Sew the seams.
❖ *If your lining is made from two pieces of fabric:* Straight-stitch (see page 16) down the sides, starting from the spot you marked and sewing down and around the curve, if you made one, across the bottom and up the other side, ending at the other marked point. Sew back and forth for a few stitches at the start and end of the seam to reinforce it.
❖ *If your bag is made from a single piece of fabric:* Straight-stitch down one side, starting from the spot you marked and sewing down and around the first curve, if you made one, ending right on the edge of the fold. Repeat the process on the other edge of the bag. Sew back and forth for a few stitches at the start and end of each seam to reinforce it. If you've made curved corners, cut away the excess fabric 5 mm (¼ inch) from the stitching.
To make the outside of the bag, repeat steps 1 and 2 with the outer fabric.

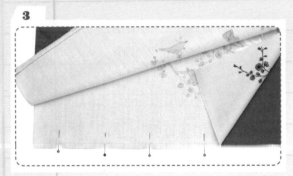

3 Turn the outer piece of fabric right side out and place it inside the lining piece – the lining piece should still be inside out. Pin the lining and the outer piece together along the top edge on one side of the bag, then straight-stitch 5 mm (¼ inch) down from top, the whole way across. Turn the bag over and repeat for the other top edge.

4 Turn the whole thing right side out through one of the side holes.

5 Press the top edges flat. Along the side gaps, pin the lining and outer fabric of the side gaps together, folding the two raw edges under and straight-stitching close to the edge.

6 Put one handle in place then fold the top opening over 5 cm (2 inches), and pin. With the handle still in place, straight-stitch to create the casing, pulling the fabric flat as you go. The fabric will gather naturally off the ring. Repeat for the second handle and your bag is complete.

4

5

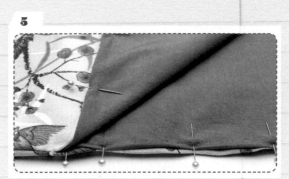

6

27 leather clutch

Does your old leather jacket speak a little too loudly of a trend long since past? Rather than feel guilty about no longer loving it, why not reuse that leather by chopping it up and converting it into a clutch? There's no need to buy an expensive designer clutch when you've got a whole chunk of unloved leather at your disposal.

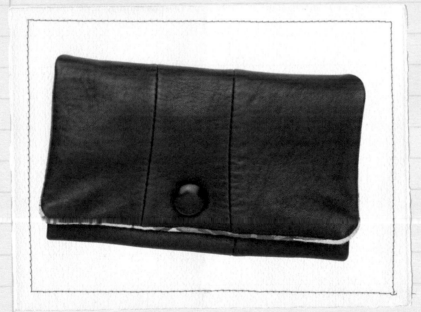

WHAT YOU NEED

- ▸ OUTDATED AND UNLOVED LEATHER JACKET
- ▸ MASKING TAPE
- ▸ SILVER OR GOLD PEN
- ▸ NYLON OR UPHOLSTERY THREAD

- ▸ FABRIC FOR LINING – thicker fabric (such as upholstery fabric, thickish linen or thickish satin) is better, to give the clutch more structure

- ▸ LEATHER NEEDLES – one for your sewing machine, and one for hand stitching
- ▸ SCISSORS
- ▸ MEASURING TAPE

HOW TO MAKE IT

1 Cut the side front panel out of the jacket, cutting as close to the button edge as possible. Leave the pocket lining intact, but remove any other lining and save it for another project.

2 To mark out your leather rectangle, measure from the bottom of the pocket to as close as possible to the bottom of the jacket, and draw a line that runs parallel to the pocket. Measure out from either sides of the pocket, using even measurements if possible, and mark lines at right angles to the pocket. With the pocket facing down, fold over the top flap and mark a line where you'd like the flap to sit, allowing 5 mm (¼ inch) for the seam. Make sure all your angles are at 180 degrees, so your rectangle won't be wonky, then cut the leather rectangle out.

3 Cut a piece of lining approximately 2.5 cm (1 inch) larger all round than the piece of leather – this will cover any unexpected stretching or warping as you sew. Place two the two pieces together, with right sides facing, and use small strips of masking tape to secure them place – you can remove these as you sew.

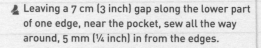 **4** Leaving a 7 cm (3 inch) gap along the lower part of one edge, near the pocket, sew all the way around, 5 mm (¼ inch) in from the edges.

5 Trim any excess fabric from around the edges and turn the whole thing right side out.

6 Turn up the bottom flap, and flip over the top flap to make sure you're happy with the way things are sitting. (Make sure, too, that when you sew up the side seams, you can put your hand down into the pocket properly – that is, you haven't reoriented the whole thing so that you end up putting your hand up into the pocket.) Hand-stitch the two sides together (sewing through the edges of the lining fabric, rather than the leather), using ladder stitch (see page 21). Stitch a button on the flap to match your lining, or use one of the buttons off the jacket. Stitch one part of a snap fastener to the underside of the flap, through the lining fabric only. Using the leather needle, stitch the other part of the snap to the leather.

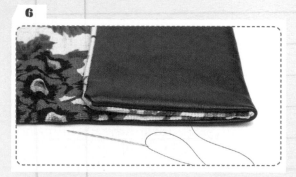

A lady's jacket will be more tailored and have less leather to work with than a man's, so it may not be possible to have an even spacing of leather on either side of your pocket. Either use a man's jacket if this bothers you, or make the unevenness a feature.

TIPS FOR WORKING WITH LEATHER

* *Loosen the tension on your sewing machine – a domestic machine will be able to handle one layer of leather plus lining.*
* *Use leather needles.*
* *Use a walking foot on your machine if possible. If not, the standard all-purpose foot will be fine.*
* *Use a longer stitch length.*
* *Don't pin the leather! Once leather is pierced, the holes will remain. To secure two pieces together, use bulldog clips or masking tape that can be easily removed.*
* *Take your time when sewing. Again, there's no going back and unpicking.*

* *Sew with the fabric side down and the leather facing up. Otherwise, the feed dogs on your machine will scratch the leather.*
* *Nylon or upholstery thread is ideal, but standard sewing thread will be okay for smaller projects, as many machines can't handle the thicker thread. Use nylon or upholstery thread for the side seams when hand-stitching.*
* *As you are sewing, soft leather will want to stretch and warp, so try to hold it straight as you feed it through the machine.*

For a fancier finish, flip the flap up at an angle to show off a wedge of the lining fabric, carefully hand sew along the edge using the leather needle and small stitches, and add a button of your choice.

28 iPad jacket

Stand out from the crowd with a customised iPad jacket. You'll be the envy of geeks and hipsters alike, and can smile smugly knowing that no-one else will have one like yours.

This project uses an old lined suit jacket. The shaping in some jackets means it may not be possible to line up a checked pattern neatly. Look closely at this before you start, or just accept that the pattern (if the jacket has one) may not align.

WHAT YOU NEED

- IPAD (25.5 cm x 20 cm; if you want to make a jacket for a different tablet computer or e-reader, adjust the measurements accordingly)
- SUIT JACKET WITH LINING
- SEWING MACHINE

- SCISSORS
- NEEDLE AND THREAD
- PINS AND RULER
- TAILOR'S CHALK/DISAPPEARING INK MARKER PEN
- BATTING OF MEDIUM THICKNESS,

(measuring 29.5 cm x 44 cm; or use the measurement of your tablet and add 4 cm (for the seam) to the width measurement, double the length measurement and add 4 cm (for the seam allowance)

HOW TO MAKE IT

BEFORE

1

1 Lay the jacket out sideways on a table and position the iPad so the bottom (or the shortest edge) aligns parallel to the bottom edge of the jacket, and 1.5 cm (5/8 inch) in. Flip the side of the jacket over the iPad. This will become the flap of the cover, so adjust it so that it sits in a way that looks good to you. (If you have a protective cover for your iPad and want to always keep this on, bear in mind that the iPad jacket will be a little looser if you plan to use it without the protective iPad cover.)

2

3

2 Measure 3 cm out from the right-hand side of the iPad and mark a line in the lining fabric. Measure 21.5 cm (8½ inches) from the bottom of the iPad, and mark a line on the lining fabric.

3 Cut along these lines so you end up with a rectangle.

4 Unpick any darts in that section of the fabric, but leave any seams, and press flat with an iron, if the fabric will stand it.

5 Cut a piece of batting (see 'What you need' instructions). Lift the lining up and insert the batting.

4

5

6 On both open sides, fold the lining under 1.5 cm (⅝ inch), and do the same with the outer fabric. Pin these edges together and straight-stitch (or hand-stitch if you prefer, see page 16) 5 mm (¼ inch) from the edges.

7 Position the iPad on the fabric, and fold the bottom up. Fold the top flap over to check that you are happy with the flap length, and pin the sides in place.

8 Using ladder stitch (see page 21), stitch both sides sides up. Add a button to match up with any buttonholes. If buttons aren't your thing, stitch the buttonhole up and attach Velcro to the underside of the flap instead. You could add ribbon, a fabric flower, or any other embellishment to the cover as an alternative. It doesn't have to be all work and no play!

29 iPhone case

A vintage-inspired case for a modern device, embracing the now with a gentle nod to a bygone era. This seems like a lengthy task, but is actually pretty easy. Once you've got the hang of it, you'll want to make one for all your friends.

WHAT YOU NEED

▶ IPHONE OR OTHER SMARTPHONE
▶ A SMALL PIECE OF VINTAGE FABRIC
  (I used 1960s curtain fabric)
▶ A SMALL PIECE OF FABRIC FOR LINING
  (cotton is good, as it's sturdy and easy
  to sew)
▶ VINTAGE BUTTON
▶ A SMALL PIECE OF MEDIUM-
  THICKNESS FUSIBLE INTERFACING
  (see glossary on page 146)
▶ RIBBON –10 cm (4 inches) long and
  about 2.5 cm (1 inch) wide
▶ SEWING MACHINE
▶ SCISSORS
▶ NEEDLE
▶ THREAD
▶ A SMALL SQUARE OF VELCRO (Craft
  stores sell Velcro pre-cut into small
  squares – one of these is ideal)
▶ IRON
▶ TRACING PAPER, TISSUE PAPER OR
  BAKING PAPER
▶ PENCIL

HOW TO MAKE IT

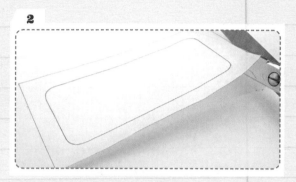

1. Place the phone onto the piece of tracing paper and trace around the outside edge.

2. Measure 1 cm (½ inch) from this line on all four sides, and draw a box around the phone outline. Cut out this template.

3. Position the template in turn onto the outer fabric, lining and interfacing, trace the outline and cut the pieces. You will need:
   2 pieces of outer fabric
   2 pieces of lining fabric
   2 pieces of fusible interfacing

4. Iron the interfacing to the wrong side of both pieces of lining.

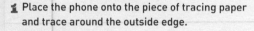

5 Lay a lining piece on top of an outer piece with the right sides together, and stitch 5 mm (¼ inch) from the top. Do the same with the other lining and outer pieces, then open them up and press flat.

6 At both ends of the ribbon, make a 5 mm (¼ inch) hem to prevent fraying. Stitch this ribbon to the piece of lining that is opposite the side you want it to fold over to, centring it on the seam and stitching 2.5 cm (1 inch) away from the seam.

7 Align the two pieces, with right sides together, making sure that the middle seams match up. Stitch up both sides, 5 mm (¼ inch) in from the edge. Don't panic if the pieces don't line up perfectly, as the seam allowance will cover this.

8 Stitch 5 mm (¼ inch) across the bottom of the outer fabric pieces, and gently round off the corners with a pair of scissors.

9 Turn the whole thing inside out, and stitch 5 mm (¼ inch) across the bottom of the lining pieces. Zigzag the edge to stop any fraying.

10 Now this is where the magic happens. Stuff the lining into the outer case – this can be quite fiddly, and you may have to use the end of a pen to push those corners right down to the bottom.

6

7
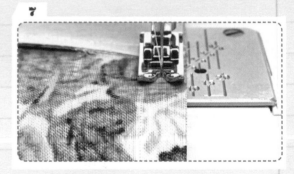

5

8
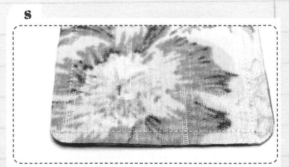

9

12

10

11 Press the whole thing flat, pop the phone in and mark the position and length you'd like the tab to sit at.

12 With the phone in its case, stick the looped side of the Velcro to the back of the ribbon, and match up the hooked part of the Velcro on the outside of the case. Take the phone out and stitch these into place. Finally, to complete the look, stitch a vintage button to your ribbon tab.

11

BITS &
PIECES

FABRIC TYPES AND CARE

FABRIC TYPES

Fabrics can be woven (such as linen, wool, cotton); knitted (jersey, lycra and many other stretch fabrics); formed into sheets (plastics, vinyls and synthetic fabrics); or made from skins (leather and furs). The following are some of the most common types of fabric that you'll encounter in fabric stores or second-hand and charity stores.

ABOUT FIBRES AND FABRICS

Fibres can be natural or synthetic. Natural fibres can be derived from either plants (such as linen, cotton and hemp) or animals (including silk, wool, alpaca, cashmere and angora). Synthetic fabrics include lycra, nylon, rayon, vinyl and polyester.

A fabric can be described according to its composition or the way it's spun, finished or treated. For example, silk, cotton, linen and rayon are all types of fibres, while satin, velvet and damask are types of weaves. Therefore it's possible to have silk damask, linen damask, cotton damask, rayon satin, silk satin, silk velvet and cotton velvet, among many other possibilities.

CALICO

Calico is a plain-woven cotton fabric, usually unbleached and stiff. It's often used for toiles (see glossary) and craft projects such as tote bags, as it is inexpensive and sturdy. Calico originated in Calicut, India, and is one of the oldest cottons.

CARING FOR CALICO Warm machine-wash, hot iron. Printed designs on calico may fade or run when washed.

CASHMERE

Cashmere is a light yet luxurious and warm fibre from the Cashmere goat. It has been woven into shawls known as pashminas since as far back as the 11th century. Prince released a great song in 1993, called 'Pink Cashmere'.

CARING FOR CASHMERE Carefully hand-wash using wool detergent and cool or lukewarm water. Roll in a towel, press to remove excess water, then lay flat to dry on a towel or a drying rack.

CHIFFON

Chiffon is a very fine, sheer silk or synthetic fibre, mostly used for evening wear, wedding dresses, lingerie, and embellishments such as ruffles and gathers. The word is French and means 'rag', but ironically this fabric was an indicator of wealth and status throughout Europe from the 1700s onwards.

CARING FOR CHIFFON Chiffon is very fragile and prone to tearing, especially when wet. Hand-wash in light liquid detergent and cold water, or preferably dry clean. Don't rub any stains, as this may irreparably damage the fabric.

CHINTZ

Chintz is a cotton fabric with a glazed sheen, mainly used for soft furnishings and draperies because of its dirt-resistant properties. The word chintz is derived from the Hindi *chint*, meaning 'gaudily printed fabric'. It originated in India, and the first designs featured brightly coloured exotic birds and flowers painted onto calico.

CARING FOR CHINTZ A washing machine will damage the glaze on chintz, so dry cleaning is recommended, or gentle hand-washing.

CORDUROY

Corduroy is a vertically ribbed, durable but soft cotton fabric. It was first worn by kings and the name comes from the French *corps du roi*, meaning 'king's body'; it later became known as 'poor man's velvet' when worn by workers and students.

CARING FOR CORDUROY Corduroy is quite a sturdy fabric, but take care to iron on the reverse side to avoid crushing and marking the pile.

DENIM

Denim is a hard-wearing cotton twill (see glossary) fabric, synonymous with jeans. It originated in the French town of Nimes, and has a phenomenal history spanning slave labour, Genoese sailors in the 1500s (the word 'jeans' derives from 'Genoa'), factory workers during World War II, American pop culture in the 1950s, right through to the continuing styles and trends today.

CARING FOR DENIM Denim will gradually fade over time, but can be washed and tumble dried with minimal shrinkage.

DUPIONI

Dupioni silk is a shimmery but rough woven fabric, with pronounced bumps at random intervals. The irregular texture is produced when two or more silkworms spin their cocoons too closely together, causing the fibres to interlock.

CARING FOR DUPIONI Dry clean only, as washing will cause it to shrink and lose its shimmery effect.

GABARDINE

Gabardine is a tough fabric with a pronounced tight weave, traditionally made from wool, and commonly used to make suits and overcoats. It was invented by the founder of the well-known fashion label Burberry in 1879, and worn by Ernest Shackleton on his Antarctic expedition in 1914.

CARING FOR GABARDINE Dry clean only.

GEORGETTE

Georgette is a sheer and lightweight crepe-like silk, rayon or polyester fabric, often used in wedding dresses and formal wear. It's named after the the early-20th-century French fashion designer and dressmaker Madame Georgette de la Plante.

CARING FOR GEORGETTE Hand-wash in cold water using a mild detergent, or dry clean.

JERSEY

Jersey is a fine stretch-knit fabric, most often used to make t-shirts and draped garments such as dresses and tops. Coco Chanel caused controversy in 1916 by using jersey in a range of suits, at a time when it was only worn as underwear.

CARING FOR GABARDINE Some varieties can be machine-washed, others need dry cleaning – consult a dry cleaner before proceeding.

LEATHER

Leather is a natural material derived from the skin of an animal, mainly cows and pigs. Leather dates back to prehistoric times when humans used skins as clothing and shelter. Over time tanning processes and the growth of industrialisation led to its widespread use not only in fashion but also cars, furnishings, tools and machinery.

CARING FOR LEATHER Think of leather as skin when caring for it – clean it very gently with a damp cloth and mild soapy water, or use a product designed for leather. Pat dry and allow to dry completely out of sunlight and away from heat sources. When it's dry, gently rub in some leather conditioner using a soft cloth (make sure you apply the conditioner to the cloth first, not the leather). This step will prolong the life of your garment.

LINEN

Linen is a natural fibre made from flax, and is lightweight, durable and breathable. The oldest of all woven fabrics, linen dates back to prehistory. It was used in ancient Greece, Egyptian mummies were wrapped in it, the Phoenicians introduced it to Ireland, and it's still widely used today for all manner of household and wearable items.

CARING FOR LINEN Machine-wash (it can withstand high temperatures), and lay flat to dry. Using a hot iron, iron while still damp.

MOHAIR

Mohair is a strong, hairy and sometimes rough fibre from the hair of the Angora goat. Kid mohair, which is taken from very young animals, is the softest, finest, least hairy type. The Ankara region in Turkey was the main producer of mohair until about 1850. Now Angora goats are farmed around the world. (Confusingly, the fibre known as angora does not come from Angora goats, but Angora rabbits.)

CARING FOR MOHAIR Hand-wash in lukewarm water, roll in a towel to squeeze out excess moisture and dry flat.

NYLON

Nylon is a tough, lightweight synthetic fibre, famously used for stockings, but also for sportswear and underwear. Nylon was developed by Dupont in 1935, and soon afterwards nylon stockings were introduced to stores in New York.

CARING FOR NYLON Machine- or hand-wash.

ORGANZA

Organza is a sheer, light and stiff fabric, traditionally made from silk, but now also from synthetics. It's mostly used in wedding dresses, evening wear and trimmings. The name is derived from that of Urgang, an ancient town in Turkestan famed for its silk market.

CARING FOR ORGANZA Dry clean only or you may lose the crispness.

POLYESTER

Polyester is a strong synthetic fibre and a by-product of petroleum. It was introduced in the early 1950s, and in an economy focused on speed and convenience, it immediately became the fabric of choice due to for its wash-and-wear and wrinkle-free properties. Textile mills began popping up throughout America, including at such locations as old gas stations.

CARING FOR POLYESTER Wash inside out to prevent pilling. Cool iron.

RAYON

Also known as viscose, rayon is a versatile, semi-synthetic manufactured fibre, often blended with other fibres and widely used in all manner of apparel and soft furnishings because its properties are similar to those of natural fibres – namely, comfort and breathability.

Rayon rose to popularity between the 1930s and 1950s with the introduction of the Hawaiian shirt.

CARING FOR RAYON Hand-wash or gentle machine-wash using a mild detergent. Cool iron.

SATIN

Satin is a glossy woven fabric with a dull backing, and is made in varying types, thicknesses and weights. Traditionally satin was made of silk, and as a luxurious and expensive fabric, was used only by the upper classes. The name is derived from the shipping port known in medieval times as Zaitun (now Quanzhou), in China.

CARING FOR SATIN If the satin is made of silk, then dry clean only. A synthetic blend may be machine-washed on a gentle cycle with cool water and a mild detergent; if you're unsure of the composition, a professional cleaner will be able to identify the fibre for you.

SUEDE

Suede is the natural napped underside of the leather from lamb, calf or pig, and is less durable but softer than standard leather. The word suede is derived from the French *gants de Suède*, which means 'gloves of Sweden' – the most common form of luxury imports into France in the 19th century.

CARING FOR SUEDE As it is porous, suede can quickly absorb moisture and become dirty. Prevention is better than the cure, so take care to regularly protect it with a silicone suede protection spray. Clean any dirt off when the suede is dry, using a suede brush and brushing in one direction only.

SYNTHETIC OR FAUX FUR

Made from synthetic fibres, faux fur is designed to resemble (and is often indistinguishable from) genuine fur. It was introduced in the 1920s due to the scarcity and expense of the real thing, and later became popular as an alternative to killing animals for their pelts.

CARING FOR FAUX FUR Either spot clean with a damp cloth, or gentle hand-wash in cool water with a mild detergent. Squeeze out excess water with a towel but do not tumble dry – let it dry naturally, then fluff it up gently with a brush.

TWEED

Tweed is a roughly woven woollen fabric, with a plain or twill weave or sometimes a checked pattern. Tweed is historically associated with hunting and other country sports in the United Kingdom, but over the years it has also made its way into high-end fashion collections.

CARING FOR TWEED Dry clean or gently hand-wash in cool water with a wool detergent. Dry flat to maintain the shape of the garment.

VELVET

Velvet fabric has a pile weave, and a soft, downy, plush texture. Once reserved for the elite and nobility, luxurious velvet symbolised wealth and power. Italy was the largest producer of velvet between the 12th and 18th centuries, supplying it to other European countries.

CARING FOR VELVET Dry clean only, or gently blot stains with a damp cloth and mild detergent. Blot dry and repeat until stain is removed. Avoid rubbing; this will damage the pile. Velvet 'bruises' easily, so avoid folding it if you can. Uncut velvet is best stored on a roll; alternatively, fold it as little as possible and interleave the layers with tissue paper to soften the creases.

GLOSSARY

Appliqué Fabric shapes sewn onto a background fabric, by hand or machine, as decoration. See page 80.

Backstitch One or two firm stitches taken at the beginning or end of a row of stitching to reinforce and secure. See page 20.

Bar tacks A series of hand- or machine-made stitches, used for reinforcing areas of stress, such as pocket openings or buttonholes. See page 19.

Baste To sew with large running stitches, or a long machine-stitch, to hold two or more layers of fabric together temporarily (see also Tack). See page 19.

Batting A layer of insulating material – commonly cotton, wool, polyester or a blend of these – between two layers of fabric. Also known as wadding.

Bezel A metal or plastic rim into which a jewel, bead or other embellishment is set.

Bias An imaginary line at 45 degrees to the straight grain of a fabric; the bias stretches more than the straight grain (see also Grain).

Bias binding Stretchy tape made from strips of fabric cut on the bias with both long edges folded in; it may be commercial or homemade. Used for binding or facing seams, hems, armholes and the like. See page 13.

Bind To finish the raw edge of a garment by attaching a narrow strip of fabric that then folds over to enclose the raw edge.

Blind stitch A stitch used for catching the fabric of a hem to the garment, so that the stitching is invisible on the right side of the garment. See ladder stitch page 21.

Bobbin Round metal or plastic spool holding the thread that forms the underside of a machine stitch.

Bodice The top half of a dress, between shoulders and waist, or hips, with or without sleeves.

Casing A flat tube of fabric (either a double hem or an additional piece of fabric) through which cord, ribbon or elastic can be threaded, for example to draw in the waistline of a garment.

Chalk pencil Used for marking fabric with a fine, accurate line (see also Tailor's chalk).

Clip To make small cuts into the seam allowance on a curved seam, as far as (but not through) the stitching, so the seam will lie flat. See page 15.

Dart A triangular or diamond-shaped tuck, stitched into a garment to give it a more precise shape. See page 8.

Disappearing ink marker pens Air- or water-soluble ink pens for marking fabric with sewing lines or embroidery designs (see also Chalk pencil).

Drawstring A cord or ribbon that is inserted through a hem or casing to draw up fullness or create a closure on a garment.

Dressmaker's pencil A fine chalk pencil used to mark lines on fabric. They come in various colours (see also Tailor's chalk).

Facing A piece of fabric that neatens and finishes the raw edge of a garment, such as a neck edge, the front of a jacket or an armhole edge; it can be cut separately or formed by folding the fabric back on itself.

Fastener Any type of garment closure, such as a zipper, hook and eye, snap fastener, button, Velcro or the like.

Feed dogs Saw-shaped teeth that grip and move fabric under the sewing machine presser foot.

Findings Any metal or plastic bits and pieces used in the making of, for example, jewellery.

Finger-press To use finger pressure only to mark a fold or open a seam.

Finish To neaten a raw edge and prevent fraying by turning it under and stitching it in place, or by zigzagging, overlocking, overcasting or binding.

French curve/seamstress curve A flat piece of plastic with curved edges, used to mark out curved areas in patterns.

Fuse To join two surfaces together by the use of fusible webbing or fusible interfacing, which have heat-activated glue on one or both sides.

Fusible webbing Heat-activated adhesive product with glue on one or both sides, used to stabilise or bond fabric surfaces. Fusible webbing comes in narrow rolls (for hems) and paper-backed sheets (for appliqué). See page 10 and 15.

Gather To draw up fabric with rows of machine- or hand-stitching to make it narrower.

Grade (or Layer) To trim the raw edges of seam allowances to graduated widths to reduce bulk and avoid ridges. See page 15.

Grain Direction of woven fabric threads: the straight grain runs parallel to the selvedge; the opposite grain runs at right angles to the selvedge and has slightly more give than the straight grain (see also Bias).

Hem (noun) a finished lower edge of a garment; or (verb) to finish a raw edge by turning it under once, then usually once again, and stitching the folded edge in place by hand or machine.

Hemline The line formed by the lower edge of a garment; or the line on a paper pattern showing where the hem is to be folded up.

Interfacing Woven or non-woven (bonded) material used to stabilise and give body to fabric; available in a variety of weights, thicknesses and degrees of flexibility, as well as in fusible or sewn-in forms. See page 15.

Ladder stitch A hand stitch worked back and forth between two folded finished edges to join them with an invisible, flat seam. See page 21.

Layer See Grade.

Lining Separate layer of fabric attached inside a garment, used to increase comfort and durability, add weight and warmth and/or conceal raw edges.

Machine basting The longest straight stitch on the sewing machine; used to hold sections of fabric together temporarily during construction.

Nap (or Pile) The raised surface on certain types of fabric (such as velvet or corduroy), which gives direction by causing shading on the fabric. It is important to cut napped fabric with all the pattern pieces lying in the same direction.

Needles Hand-sewing needles are made of steel with an eye at one end and a point at the other. They come in a variety of shapes and sizes, depending on their function. Machine-sewing needles have the eye near the point and a shank section that is flat on one side and fits into the needle clamp on the machine.

Non-woven Fabric not made of thread or yarn; can be natural (such as suede or leather) or synthetic (such as vinyl and some bonded interfacings).

Overcast To stitch over a raw edge by hand or machine to prevent fraying. See page 10.

Overlock To sew, finish and simultaneously trim a seam using a specialised sewing machine known as an overlocker.

Pivot To leave the needle in the fabric after sewing, raise the presser foot and turn the fabric to a different angle; then lower the presser foot and continue to sew.

Pleat Sewn-down fold in fabric, of varying widths. Pleats give fullness while reducing bulk.

Press To use an iron; to prevent distortion and stretching during construction of a garment, the iron should not, however, be moved back and forth as in ironing, but rather placed on the fabric, then lifted and moved.

Presser foot Removable part of the sewing machine that holds the fabric in place against the feed dogs when sewing.

Pressing cloth A plain fabric cloth, used between the iron and delicate fabrics to protect them. Or simply use a clean scrap of undyed cloth, a handkerchief or even a piece of baking paper.

Raw edge Cut, unfinished edge of fabric, which can fray easily.

Ruche To gather up, usually on a section of a garment.

Ruffle Strip of fabric, gathered or finely pleated onto a garment.

Running stitch A simple stitch made by running the thread in and out of the fabric. Used for tacking and for gathering, and in embroidery. See page 19.

Seam (or Seam line) The line of hand or machine stitching joining two pieces of fabric.

Seam allowance The margin of fabric outside the stitched seam line; normally 15 mm ($\frac{5}{8}$ inch) in commercial patterns.

Seam ripper Small pointed tool with a sharp blade, used for unpicking seams or cutting stitches; also known as an unpicker or 'quick unpick'.

Selvedge The woven edge along the sides of a width of fabric. Selvedges don't fray. They shrink at a greater rate than the rest of the fabric, though, so they should be cut off and not incorporated into garments.

Shirring Rows of gathering in a garment, where a fine elastic is used in the bobbin instead of normal thread; the resulting gathers are therefore stretchy. See page 32.

Slipstitch Used for joining two folded edges from the right side, slipstitch is worked as invisibly as possible, taking very small stitches through each fold of fabric alternately.

Stay-stitching A line of machine stitching just inside the seam line on curved edges that stabilises and keeps the curve from distorting.

Tack To use long machine- or hand-stitches to temporarily mark positions or sew pieces together before they are permanently stitched; the tacking is then removed. Tacking is also known as basting.

Tailor's chalk Small, sharp-edged piece of hard chalk used to make temporary markings on fabric (see also Chalk pencil).

Tension The pressure placed on the upper and lower threads as they are fed through a sewing machine; when the tension is set perfectly, the link between the upper and lower threads is in the centre of the fabric layers.

Toile A test version of a garment, made up in inexpensive fabric, so that the pattern can be adjusted before the actual fabric is cut.

Topstitch To make a line of hand or machine stitching (decorative or functional) on the right side of the work, at a measured distance from finished edges or seams.

Trim To remove excess seam allowance or fabric with scissors. Also a generic term for items such as braid, ribbon, cord or lace, used to embellish a project.

Tuck A fold or a pleat in fabric that is usually sewn in place. See page 8.

Turn out (also Turn right side out) To turn the right side of a project or section to the outside, after sewing it on the wrong side.

Twill A type of textile weave with a pattern of diagonal parallel ribs

Unpicker See Seam ripper.

Velcro Registered trade name of nylon hook-and-loop fastener tape.

Wadding See Batting.

Walking foot A sewing machine attachment to allow for sewing through several layers of fabric without shifting the lower and upper fabrics; useful for slippery fabrics or those that might be scratched by the feed dogs, such as leather.

Woven Describing fabric that is created from yarn by a weaving process, as opposed to non-woven.

Yoke A fitted, flat section of a garment, from which the remainder of the garment hangs; usually across the shoulders of a shirt or the waist of a skirt.

Zigzag A machine stitch that goes from side to side, producing a serrated effect; useful for finishing raw edges.

Zipper foot Removable sewing machine foot that accommodates the teeth of a zipper on one side, making insertion easier. Special zipper feet are available for inserting invisible zippers.

RESOURCES

CRAFTUMI
www.craftumi.com.au

EBAY
www.ebay.com

ETSY
www.etsy.com

LINCRAFT
www.lincraft.com.au

RED CROSS
www.redcross.org.au

RETRO AGE VINTAGE FABRIC
www.vintagefabrics.com.au

SPOTLIGHT
www.spotlight.com.au

ST VINCENT DE PAUL SOCIETY
www.vinnies.org.au

**THE SALVATION ARMY
- SALVOS STORES**
www.salvos.org.au/stores

THE SMITH FAMILY
www.thesmithfamily.com.au

VINTAGE FABRIC ADDICT
www.vintagefabricaddict.com

Published in 2012 by Murdoch Books Pty Limited

Murdoch Books Australia
Pier 8/9
23 Hickson Road
Millers Point NSW 2000
Phone: +61 (0) 2 8220 2000
Fax: +61 (0) 2 8220 2558
www.murdochbooks.com.au
info@murdochbooks.com.au

Murdoch Books UK Limited
Erico House, 6th Floor
93–99 Upper Richmond Road
Putney, London SW15 2TG
Phone: +44 (0) 20 8785 5995
Fax: +44 (0) 20 8785 5985
www.murdochbooks.co.uk
info@murdochbooks.co.uk

For Corporate Orders & Custom Publishing contact Noel Hammond,
National Business Development Manager Murdoch Books Australia

Publisher: Tracy Lines
Designer: Miriam Steenhauer
Photographer: Amanda McKittrick
Project Editor: Kit Carstairs
Editor: Janine Flew
Production: Mike Crowton

National Library of Australia Cataloguing-in-Publication Data

A catalogue record for this book is available from the British Library.

Printed by 1010 Printing International Limited, China.

ABOUT THE AUTHOR

Amanda McKittrick, (known to friends as 'Kitty') has loved to combine the old with the new for as long as she is able to remember. Her life-long interest in craft, design and photography combined with nearly a decade in publishing, working on a wide range of titles, encouraged her to develop and share her passion for all things crafty.

Being a self taught crafter, Amanda wanted to create a book that provided practical insights and advice to inspire others to develop their skills, and confidence, so they too could create wonderfully-quick and inexpensive projects, and most importantly learn and have fun along the way.

ACKNOWLEDGEMENTS

This book would have been difficult to produce without the support of many.

First and foremost, thank you to my better half, Anton, for providing unwavering love, encouragement and laughs throughout the whole process – not only acting as my project manager, but also cooking, cleaning and keeping my life on track while I worked late into the night and over weekends.

Thank you to Publishing Director Chris Rennie, for granting me a brief hiatus from my office role, and sending me off on this adventure with great enthusiasm and confidence.

A huge thank you to Diana Hill and Juliet Rogers for initially considering me for this task, for giving me the opportunity and for trusting in my ability – it's great to be recognised by women I hold in high regard.

Behind every great book is a great editor – Janine Flew, the unsung hero of many a great title, not only editor extraordinaire, but a very skilled crafter who contributed far more than one could ever hope for from an editor. Thank you for wrangling my words and thoughts.

Thank you to the wonderful designer Miriam Steenhauer for bringing words and pictures to life with your unique sense of style.

And of course, the great team at Murdoch Books: Tracy Lines, Kit Carstairs, Joan Beal, Mike Crowton, Ashlea Wallington and all those who supported me with their kind words.

Thanks to Mum, Dad, Grace, Grandad and Aunty Catherine for your love, and especially Grace, who selflessly lent me her camera for the duration of this project.

To my friends who have felt neglected while I worked on this book, thanks for your patience and understanding. Special thanks to Kate Fitzgerald for invaluable feedback, honesty and inspiration, and to Heather Menzies for regularly sending me hand-written letters of encouragement and keeping me laughing.

And last but certainly not least, a big fluffy meow to my Crafty Kittens Club – Janine Flew, Miriam Steenhauer (Mimsy), Kate Green (CK), Kate Wheeler (Squeels) and Kate Fitzgerald (Fitzy) – thanks for keeping me laughing and inspired. I'm so blessed to be able to share life, love and craft with you ladies.